How to Create a Life You Love

No Magical Thinking Required

Jason McBride

ISBN: 979-8-9950230-0-5 (Hardback)

ISBN: 979-8-9950230-1-2 (Paperback)

ISBN: 979-8-9950230-2-9 (Ebook)

ISBN: 979-8-9950230-3-6 (Audiobook)

For K, C, G, & T—you four are my everything

Also by Jason McBride

Haiku Comics Collections:

Wild Divinity

Haiku Comics from the Anthropocene

Twisted Haiku Series:

Pirate Haiku

Horror Haiku

Sci-Fi Haiku

Zines:

Surreal Haiku: I Stare at the Sea

Surreal Haiku: The Joy of Nothing

Weirdoku: A Disciple of the Sea

Near Future Cosmic Tales

Quantum Joy Infinite Melancholy

Contents

Introduction

Are you human? We live in a world where we must now prove to robots that we are human to get access to our online accounts because some malevolent humans have unleashed robot armies to steal our data, information, and attention.

The target of many robots in the service of rogue tech oligarchs is to rob us of our very humanity. Every day, you prove to robots that you are human by clicking pictures or performing other menial tasks. When was the last time you proved to yourself that you are human?

Ever since I was in high school, I've been fascinated by Ralph Waldo Emerson, Henry David Thoreau, and the other transcendentalists (Thank you, Miss Taggart!). As a teenager, I was drawn to their rebellion against the immoral exercise of authority and desire to live free of absurd social conventions, self-seriousness, and herd mentality. Now that I stand in the middle of middle age, I'm drawn to their call to be human. Emerson and Thoreau weren't worried about optimization; they were too busy trying to connect deeply with nature because to be human is to seek unification with the natural world.

Somewhere between high school and now, I fell under the spell of haiku poetry. My creative work for the past ten years has been using haiku as a tool for uncovering what it means to live a human life. Since the artificial rise of artificial intelligence in the past three years, this work has taken on greater urgency.

I don't want to be a robot. I want to be human. I'm not a technophobe, but I am willing to take a Luddite-like hammer to our algorithmic overlords who try to steal our humanity for the sake of enriching a few billionaires with a startling lack of reading comprehension.

The essays in this collection were published online between February 2024 and December 2025. They are all explorations of one question: What does it mean to live a deeply human life? These essays are all illustrated with poetry comics. It would've been much easier to publish this collection without the comics. But when I created a manuscript without illustrations, I felt that I had stripped out the soul of the essays. For me, to be deeply human means to be a little weird. It means to combine things that you might not think belong together, like poetry, comics, and prose.

The other thread that connects all of these essays is my belief that, as humans, we do not need magical thinking to solve our problems. We need creativity, grit, and curiosity.

These illustrated essays are how I prove to myself that I am human. They are my effort at effecting powerful changes in my life. I hope they are useful to you in your quest to live the most human life you can.

Because I am obsessed with being human, I have not used AI in any part of this book. This book comes from my head and heart, which are filled with the thoughts of thousands of other writers and artists. It was written by me, without the help of AI. The art is from my hands, without any aid from AI. The editing was done by humans. This book is not perfect. Despite the best efforts of my editorial team and me, a few mistakes will have inevitably slipped through. I hope you will see these blemishes as evidence of the human origin of this book, and not as marks of carelessness.

This book is not my final word on the question of what it looks like to live a deeply human life. I am the *Deeply Human Life* columnist for Medium.com (self-appointed), where I write illustrated essays at least once a week. I also write a freemium newsletter (90% of the posts are free to everyone) called *Weirdo Poetry*, where I get more personal and share poems, poetry comics, animations, illustrated essays, and other madness about my own quest for the deeply human life, and share about my creative process as it evolves.

You can explore the *Weirdo Poetry* newsletter at *WeirdoPoetry.-Substack.com.*

This book will no doubt be categorized as "self-help" in the bookstores. But I hope that you will find it useful not as a book of answers but as a book that challenges you to ask better questions. I hope that it sparks an unquenchable desire to prove to yourself that you are human.

In the end, we each only have this one life. Why not live it in the most human ways possible?

Chapter 1

How to Pay Attention

Meditation is often seen as the gateway to mindfulness. It's seen as "the right way" to enter the pathway of paying attention. Meditation is also often used as a shorthand for mindfulness. However, meditation is only one tool for building mindfulness, and it's not a tool that works for everyone.

The core of mindfulness is not breath-work or being still; it's noticing what you notice. It's easy to sail through life in default mode. Our brains are programmed to filter out any information not essential to our survival. However, we often do a poor job of teaching our brains what types of information we want to pay attention to.

Paying attention is a skill you must practice regularly. How do you learn to pay attention? How do you build mindfulness? What does it look like?

When you have a measure of mindfulness, you notice the food you are eating instead of mindlessly snacking throughout the day when you're stressed. You notice the creeping anxiety that comes with certain work interactions, instead of being unsure why you always come home tired and cranky.

THE SUN IS OUR CLOCK
THE NIGHT SKY IS OUR THEATER
THE SEA IS OUR GRAVE

When you read about meditation, you are most likely only learning about one particular mode of meditation: transcendental meditation. This is a form of meditation that focuses on your breathing and having a single mantra. It's a form of meditation that can cause physical pain for some, and has never worked for me. Two alternative tools I use to build mindfulness are walking and writing haiku.

For the past eight years, I have developed a creative and mindfulness practice around paying attention. I walk nearly every day, regardless of the weather, in nature or around my mid-sized town for as long as I can. After my walks, and sometimes even during my walks, I write one or more haiku poems about what I've seen.

Haiku is the poetry of observation. In traditional Japanese haiku, the poet writes about their observations of the natural world, within the context of the changing seasons, in seventeen syllables. English language haiku splits these seventeen syllables into three lines, the first and third lines having five syllables and the second line having seven syllables.

Writing haiku gives me a reason to notice what's happening outside my loud, cluttered brain. It switches my brain from default mode to observation mode. The constraints of the haiku form also force me to think more deeply about what I have observed so that I can capture the essence of the experience. Even writing a single haiku a day will change the way you view your surroundings. It connects you with the natural world. Another advantage of this practice is that it forces you to go outside. The act of moving and changing your physical environment increases your mindfulness.

Writing a haiku is a simple task. Anyone can put together three lines by counting syllables. There's no need to rhyme or worry about meter. You can even skip the syllable counting if you like and just write a short poem that can be read in a single breath. Haiku is also a discipline that makes it easy to see your improvement after just a few days of writing. You don't even have to share your mindfulness haiku with anyone. However, you should go back and reread your work. You will find patterns in both the changing of the seasons and in your moods and the topics you focus on.

You cannot walk and write haiku for long without seeing your powers of observation sharpen. You will begin to notice more as you do other activities. If you take this practice seriously enough, you may even find yourself wondering at the magnificent dramas of creatures that you had once been completely ignorant of.

As I look back on my poems from the past several years, I've noticed that I write about the return of the great horned owl to the woods by our house every fall, and the one year the owl did not return, the year of our massive wildfires, its absence was conspicuous. This year, I noticed a different owl calling from the woods; a barred owl was competing with the great horned owl for territory.

This winter, I've been taking my walks in a different part of town because of flooding in the parks I usually meander through. Looking over my haiku from the past few months, my obsession with ducks and waterfowl is apparent. I'm seeing more types of ducks than I ever knew existed in our town.

The poems and observations from these walks have prompted me to learn more about the ecology of my area and helped me feel more deeply connected to my community. While I may have once just seen ducks, I now see wood ducks, mallards, Muscovy ducks, bluebills, and many other species of ducks, some of which live here all year round and some of which only sojourn in our waterways during the winter. This noticing keeps me attached to the present and doesn't allow room for my mind to wallow in anxiety about the past and future.

Some people will find peace in focusing on their breath as they sit perfectly still. I find peace in the feeling of my feet pushing off against the ground and the sounds of birds as they paddle around a pond. While some may use the stillness of transcendental meditation to quiet their racing thoughts, I use the activity of walking and writing haiku to center my focus.

As someone who lives with ADHD and an anxiety disorder, mindfulness is not a luxury. I must maintain high levels of focus and awareness to thrive in my roles as a work-from-home father, and freelance writer and illustrator. My haiku walks have given me the space to practice paying attention and have helped me make mindfulness a way of life.

If you are looking for an alternative way to learn how to pay more attention, try writing haiku about what you experience as you move about our wondrous world.

Chapter 2

I am a Birdman!

I've always been a curious person, and for whatever reason, my brain has always been sticky. When I was a teen, my friends and many adults would tease me about all my useless knowledge as I demolished them at trivia games. I was especially good with pop culture and history.

I never bought into the idea of "useless" knowledge. Every fact I learned could connect to other facts and unlock more of the world for me. When I was younger, knowledge for knowledge's sake felt like a worthy endeavor. But now, at almost 48, I see knowledge differently.

This past week, my favorite downtown pond was full of stunning birds. There was a majestic great blue heron and a wild variety of ducks.

I whipped out my phone and took a slew of reference photos for later comics. In the middle of one of my circuits around the pond, I was stopped in mid-haiku composition by a woman with a question. I had seen her and her friend across the pond, admiring the heron.

DUCKS MUCK ABOUT POND,

OLD HERON WATCHES FROM REEDS,

TWO GEESE MAKE PIT STOP.

"Are you a birdman?" She asked.

I paused and thought for a moment, and then laughed. "I guess so."

"Oh, good! Do you know what kind of bird that is?"

I did, of course, know. It was a great blue heron, only it had tucked its magnificent neck in, so it looked a bit like a hunchback.

"Will you tell my friend?" She pointed to her companion halfway across the pond in the direction I was already headed.

As I left, the woman called out, "Helen! He knows about birds; he'll tell you all about it!"

I do not know all about birds, I grumbled to myself. Once I reached Helen, she also asked, "Are you a birdman?"

I laughed again and, while wondering if this was a foreshadowing of my old age, admitted to being a birdman. I again identified the great blue heron.

Helen asked me about the ducks. She knew about the mallard drake and asked me about the others. I happened to know all the duck species at the pond that day, and even a few fun facts. The Muscovy duck was likely an escapee from a domestic pond, as Muscovy ducks are popular pets and domesticated pond fowl, but do not live in the wild in Oregon.

What Helen thought were wood ducks were mallard hens, and you can tell by the small band of emerald green under their wings. The dark blue, almost black bird was a Greater Scaup, or bluebill, that migrates to the northern regions of the contiguous United States from Alaska and Canada in the winter.

Helen was delighted by my facts and pointed to the apartment building across the street.

"I live there, and last week I saw a bald eagle fly right by my window. It was so beautiful! You seem like the right kind of person to tell that story to."

I marveled at her encounter, and the two of us parted. I couldn't help but think, "I am a birdman!"

The limited knowledge I've gathered about birds would certainly be considered useless by many of the same people who derided all my pop culture and trivia knowledge when I was a teen. But knowing a handful of facts about birds had given me a connection to two strangers at the park, and maybe filled their day with a bit more wonder. That is the treasure of any knowledge, you can share it with others and broaden someone else's capacity to see the world differently.

As a young man, I wanted to learn everything so I could understand the rest of the universe. Now, as a very middle-aged man, I know I cannot ever learn everything. I have a much deeper understanding of the limits of my knowledge and expertise.

I still love to learn—not because I think the knowledge itself has a particular value. Instead, I now see knowledge as a way to learn more about other people. It's how this proud introvert forms meaningful human connections with strangers.

A random fact can provide a way into a professional or personal conversation. My knowledge of professional basketball recently landed me a B2B client when the discovery call turned into a passionate discussion of Klay Thomson and his father, Mychal Thomson. We barely spoke about their project on that call. But we created a bond of mutual trust and affection.

A few years ago, I spent a riveting afternoon at Disneyland talking with a retired aviation industry employee. The jumping-off point to that encounter was my knowing a bit of aviation history trivia. My interest was enough to have them share a career's worth of gossip and stories. It was much more interesting than the parade everyone else was watching.

One of the highlights of a pre-COVID era Caribbean cruise was a long conversation with a former paper salesman, who taught me things about the differences between paper sizes and usage in the United States and Europe that I still think about and use in the publishing side of my business. Mostly, I think about the ways he lit up when talking about a job he loved, and one that most people thought was boring.

Large crowds make me uncomfortable. I don't like fake people, the kind who spread toxic positivity and claim to love everyone and everything. I can be a curmudgeon. However, given a relaxed atmosphere, I can connect with just about anyone in a one-on-one conversation.

All it takes is being curious about their life and being willing to look for ways their stories connect to the reams of "useless" knowledge I've stored up over the years. Every person you encounter has the capacity to improve your life, even if all you ever share is a single conversation.

I may never know the mysteries of the universe. But, each factoid I pick up becomes the key to unlocking the mysteries of another human being—and that is the most rewarding use of knowledge I can imagine.

MINDLESSLY
DRIVING

ON WINDY
SCENIC
BACKROADS

THE JOY OF
NOTHING

Chapter 3

Daytripping

Every drive on any highway that meanders through the scarcely populated stretches of the Western United States is a pilgrimage. It's a time to sit in the sacred loneliness that is always stalking me, and a time to marvel at the infinite variety of beauty this world contains.

On this day, I'm driving to see a friend I haven't laid eyes on for a few years. We first met as young men, confident in the holiness of our mission, arrogant in our own wisdom, strength, and youth. Or perhaps, I was the only arrogant one.

Now, we are dead-center in middle age, like the dotted yellow line I follow over hill after rolling hill, and are skeptical of the holiness we once preached, humbled by life, and now meekly confident that the only joy in life is what you are willing to bring with you.

My friend is freshly in the grips of another tragic loss, and I drive past a small cemetery and country church overlooking farmland fresh out of hibernation. I've also seen plenty of death and carry a bundle of grief over my shoulder.

The next moment, I crest another hill and see the start of

grapes on one side of the road and embryonic apples on the other. The wonder of new life is on the verge of exploding.

Life and death are both the same riddle by a different name. Mysteries we must claim, even though their solutions will always elude us.

A year or more ago, I began reading Ann Collins. She writes about discovering the world around her through microseasons. Collins explains microseasons this way:

> The idea of microseasons comes from ancient Chinese farming culture dividing the year into 24 seasons, each with a poetic name according to the Sun's position and its effect on the agriculture of that region.
>
> Some time later, this way of marking time was adopted in ancient Japan, where each season was subdivided into three parts, creating a total of 72 seasons lasting about five days each.

Instead of 24 Chinese agricultural seasons or 72 Japanese microseasons, how do I make sense of the passing of time?

As a lifelong resident of the West Coast of the United States and someone who spent their teen years in Northern California, late May until mid-June, when school gets out, is Sheryl Crow weather.

In this microseason, the sun is bright, the tyranny of winter gray is once more overthrown, and the capriciousness of early spring has mostly settled down.

Right now is also a microseason of grief; grief that is independent of the weather. But, like the Sheryl Crow weather, it too will soon transition into something else.

I wonder at the beauty of the hills and sky embracing the horizon, and notice that at this moment, my grief feels a bit lighter.

All I can do is hope I can bring a touch of this wonder and lightness to my friend, so that for at least a moment, he can remember that life and death are linked and the only joy we find in this life is that which we have the courage to bring along with us, a joy that's always made stronger when we dare to share the wonder we find as we move up and down the gentle, rolling hills.

Chapter 4

Why is the Kitchen So Damn Lonely?

I don't know a lot of other stay-at-home dads. That's not true. I know *of* several stay-at-home dads, but I don't really know any—not in a way that makes me feel part of any kind of community. This isolation has three primary causes.

One: I'm an introvert and have a difficult time seeking out and befriending strangers.

Two: I grew up and lived most of my life in a high-demand religion, where I learned that God had ordained women to be caregivers and men to be breadwinners. I was taught that men just weren't capable of the kind of nurturing that came naturally to women. Fathers could never be as close to their children as mothers. Any deviance from this natural order was an affront to God.

Three: The patriarchy. There just aren't that many stay-at-home dads in the United States. Our numbers may be growing, and many men my age and younger may be breaking out of toxic masculinity and toxic religious beliefs, but male caregivers are still an oddity.

I'm not even a stay-at-home dad as much as I'm a work-from-home dad. In addition to doing the vast majority of the caregiving and housework, I also work to help support our family as a free-lance writer, illustrator, and poet-cartoonist.

I love my life most of the time, and I'm grateful that I have had this chance to be with my children as they have grown up over the past twelve years.

My oldest is nineteen, and my youngest is thirteen. My days are filled with teens coming and going. I still have to drive my younger children all over town as my older two are busy with school and work.

It sometimes feels like I spend my days being in the car, in the kitchen, and in front of my laptop. Somewhere in between, I use the bathroom, if I'm lucky. My children are wonderful company. We laugh and listen to music together. We send each other TikToks and talk politics.

I do have friends, although my two closest friends live in different states—we stay in contact with frequent phone calls and texts.

My isolation and loneliness hit me the hardest in the kitchen. Over the past twelve years, I've become a decent cook and have even created a few of my own recipes. My grilled chicken avocado salad is incredible, and I have an entire philosophy about what makes a good meatball.

Unexpectedly, cooking and baking have become creative outlets for me, especially over the past two years. But when the cooking is done and the food has been eaten, it's often just me, the dirty dishes, and the leftovers in the kitchen. Everyone else has drifted away.

Being a poet-cartoonist, I've found the best way to express the ache of being alone in the kitchen is through a poetry comic.

THE LONELY KITCHEN

The loneliness and isolation are real, but they're not the whole story. Often, I seek solitude. I live in my head; it's where my art comes together and where I create the meaning of my existence.

Even the lonely kitchen is sometimes a place of hope and healing for me. It's also a place where I dream of an escape—an escape to a place where I can devote more time and energy to my art.

I live an incredible life of joy, opportunity, and privilege. And yet, I still find myself longing for something more.

It's not that I'm ungrateful or even unfulfilled. The issue is that in our society, the work of caregiving is largely invisible. This affects women far more than it affects men. So many women have to work a full-time job away from home and then work a full-time job at home, often mothering not just their children but their spouses as well. Coming home for these women means the start of their second shift as much as it does coming back to loved ones.

We need better policies, programs, and a more supportive culture to uplift all caregivers regardless of gender, work status, and age of their charges.

For those of us who are members of the Secret Benevolent Society of Stay-at-Home Fathers, the sense that our most important work is invisible to everyone is tremendously isolating. It's difficult to talk about because many of us were socialized to ignore and suppress our feelings, and we are a small and scattered group. It also feels weird to take up this space as a man, when it's women who overwhelmingly bear the burden of invisible work. Let's face it, too many men are also huge pains in the ass, acting more like another child for their partners to care for as opposed to giving a helping heart and hand.

The last thing I want to do is pretend this is a male problem. Just like there is a human loneliness problem, not a male loneliness epidemic, the problem with caregiving is not about men, but about the way our society's structure hurts us all.

The only way out for us is to feel our feelings, talk publicly about our experiences, and create poetry comics to help us better understand our own experiences—or maybe that's just me.

DANCING
LEAVES
ESCORT

CANADA GEESE
ON THEIR FLIGHT

ACROSS
HARVEST
MOON

Chapter 5

Finding Peace by Watching Geese

The defining emotion of my early childhood was fear. My first memory is a recurring nightmare where a Lou Ferrigno-style Hulk burst out of my closet and terrorized me.

As an adult, I was diagnosed with generalized anxiety disorder. Looking back, I have probably had an anxiety disorder since I was a very young child. I was afraid of everything, and often in a debilitating state of panic. I was the child who was too sensitive and over-reacted to everything.

What the adults in my life didn't know was that I felt everything deeply—fear and pain, but also joy and love. I seemed to grow out of my fearful stage as a teen, but really, I had just learned to mask my anxieties behind humor and swagger.

The work of my adult life has been to learn how to live a fulfilling life in a world built to torment me. I have never found medications to be a helpful intervention for me. Everyone is different, and I know that for many people with mental health challenges, including my children, medications are a life-saving intervention. But my doctors and I could never land on the right combination. Instead, I have worked with therapists to build coping mechanisms. I've designed my life to allow me to flourish in a world not set up for me.

There is a beautiful flip-side to anxiety and ADHD. I have a phenomenal imagination and ability to work in stretches of hyper-focused work so long as I also create space to rest and wander.

It's not just my mind that needs to wander. Every day, I take long walks, usually in nature. Hiking alongside the Willamette River is one of my favorite pastimes. During these walks, I practice mindfulness by noticing what I notice. One of the things I notice most often is the movements of geese.

Twice a year, our Willamette River Valley sky is filled with the honking and flying chevrons of Canada geese on their migratory journey. On their way to warmer climes, the geese seem to be pulling winter behind them, ushering in the end of fall and the beginning of the long, dark, and wet winters Western Oregon is so famous for.

Our valley has plenty of friendly waterways and large fields where these flying communities can find food and rest on their northern and southern passages. These geese are tourists, not permanent residents.

Tracking their biannual passages helps me stay connected to the rhythms of nature, helping me keep my focus on the present moment and the current happenings instead of spending too much time lost in anxious memories or anxious projections.

Watching the geese also gives me a sense of my role in my community. Am I a member of the flock, or am I more like one of the local birds, curious about the visitors and eager for them to get out of my space?

The geese don't always huddle together in large flocks. Often, a handful of them will break from the rest and land in a small pond. Even after having seen thousands of Canada geese over the decades, it's always stunning to see one make a water landing. They seem to attack the water, coming in too fast, only to make the most graceful landing imaginable. Nature is truly the most skilled engineer imaginable.

Because the geese are not always here, it's sometimes easier to be in awe of their abilities and majesty than it is of the ducks that live here year-round. It's that feeling of awe and wonder that I'm chasing. Wonder is what makes me feel most human and most connected to nature. Awe is what allows me to stay grounded in the present.

The geese are my guides to mindfulness. They come in the fall and spring to reproach me for my discordant lifestyle filled with screen-time and worry. These harbingers of the extreme seasons, summer and winter, are my prophets. Their formations signal I need to repent and reset. My greatest sin is forgetting to be grateful for the magic of the small moments of each day.

The geese have many lessons to teach, lessons I'm eager to learn and relearn because the geese teach without ego. The geese are prophets who never preach. Their actions are the message.

I cannot help but stop when I hear or see the geese in flight. More often than not, I find myself grabbing my notebook to write a haiku or observation about the geese.

Their very presence pulls me out of my mind and into the real world where life is happening. To the extent that I have learned to live in the moment and to have any kind of effective mindfulness practice, it is because of the geese.

Just like the arrival of Christmas triggers some to be more gentle and kind, or the start of spring baseball pushes others to go outside and smile, the seasonal migrations of the geese are my holiday reminder to be my best self.

Because, at my core, I am a storyteller, I often create fables and parables about the geese. I get wrapped up in their dramas and love to personify these animals and imagine they have rich interior lives.

But I have never seen an anxious wild goose. They simply live. A goose eats when hungry, drinks when thirsty, takes to the sky when it's time, and lands when the skein is ready to rest.

The goose takes no thought for tomorrow and doesn't waste a second worrying about what happened yesterday.

The fall is often when my anxiety reaches its nadir. The few weeks these beautiful beasts spend passing through coincide with my greatest need for help.

And as much as I love making up stories about the geese and writing little poems about their journey, I mostly just need a reminder that life flows.

Tomorrow, the geese will be in a different field, on a different part of the river, or another body of water altogether.

Tomorrow, my life will also have moved on. I may still be in the same physical place, but metaphysically, the river of life will have kept flowing. I only have today to savor this moment.

Fear was the defining emotion of my childhood. But contentment is the lodestar of my middle age. Each day, I do my work, like the geese fly their routes, and once the work is done, I rest and release my thoughts, like the geese coming in for a landing.

And when I forget to live content in the moment, as I often do, the geese come back and remind me that the world is filled with wonder, and it is my duty to stand in awe of nature. You cannot live in doubt or fear when you watch a skein of geese, silhouetted by a full moon, pass across the Cascades. All you can do is breathe and be.

Chapter 6

How a Recovering Self-Help Addict Finds Contentment

Humans ask questions. We are an irrepressibly curious species. Some of us are also neurotic and keep asking the same two questions over and over again:

- How can I be more productive?
- How can I be happier?

The truth is, these are both the same question. The reason you want to get more done in a day is that you believe it will lead you to a financial or emotional payoff. The emotional payoff is happiness, and the financial payoff is that you can afford happiness.

All the other typical self-help topics can also be reduced to a quest for happiness, often by way of financial prosperity. We want to be thinner, healthier, and better at this or that skill because we think that will finally make us happier. We want to make friends and influence people because happy people have friends.

You probably feel like an incomplete jigsaw puzzle and are searching for the perfect missing piece to complete you. The secret to happiness is that happiness is not a destination. What you really want to feel is contentment, and contentment comes from living in the present moment and having healthy connections to other flawed people.

I'm a recovering self-help junkie. I spent many years searching for the right mindset or practice to take all of my problems away. I wanted a lottery ticket and a magic elixir to make me feel right, to feel good. I never found those things.

Like many junkies, I got started young. My dad introduced me to self-help books when I was eleven. He meant well. He got me started on the classics: *How to Win Friends and Influence People*, *Psycho-Cybernetics*, and *The Power of Positive Thinking*.

My dad didn't force me to read anything. He did encourage me, and given my desperate need for his attention and approval combined with my voracious desire to read everything I could get my hands on, I plunged into the world of self-help, ready to believe it all.

I didn't fully understand until well into adulthood that my father was miserable. He read these same books and never found solutions to his problems. I think he hoped that I might somehow uncover what he missed.

I have no idea how many self-help books and articles I have read. After a few hundred, they all blend together. I've read much more than a few hundred. No matter how successful or disciplined I became, it was never enough.

I felt like I was climbing peaks in some endless snowy wasteland. After each summit, I expected to find a reward, only to find nothing but a challenge to climb another mountain that was a little bit taller.

My self-help habit got worse after my career and business imploded. If I had jumped into the self-help deep-end at age eleven, I was now exploring the ocean floor.

I tried everything from insane routines to metaphysical manifesting, but nothing brought me any closer to happiness.

PRODUCTIVITY
IS THE
LIE THAT
CHAINS
US TO
OTHER
PEOPLE'S
DREAMS

The self-help niche that brought me the closest to peace was the modern Stoics. Unfortunately, this niche is mostly filled with men obsessed with their own importance who are chasing the success of the earnest and interesting Ryan Holiday. One point these pretenders preach is the importance of facing death. There are a variety of *memento mori* you can buy from various stoic entrepreneurs.

Memento mori is Latin for "remember death" or "remember you too will die." The ancient Stoics often kept a grisly token to remind them that death was coming for them sooner or later. Some modern Stoics will sell you a deluxe *memento mori* from their websites.

It was the way Holiday spoke about *memento mori* in his book *The Obstacle is the Way* that provided me with the epiphany that changed my life. The idea is that death should not be feared or ignored. Once you come to accept death as both natural and inevitable, you will live a better life.

This is a similar tenet to the Buddhist idea that life is suffering. The goal is not to eliminate all suffering as much as it is to accept suffering as inevitable and find peace in your life right now.

In our society, we fear death and discomfort too much. We are so reluctant to face the inevitability of death that we often don't even grieve those who pass. Instead, we attempt to move on because we have things to do.

There are so many things that need doing that we have to keep lists and use apps, notes, and calendars to keep track of all the things. We fear death because so few of us spend any time living; we're too busy doing without ever asking if we're doing anything of importance.

You don't need a weird skull coin to remind you that you are going to die. We all know this. We all feel it, even if we work to repress it. Instead of a *memento mori* to remind you of death, you need a *memento vitae* to remind you to live.

You and I are meant to have joy in this life. Children tend to naturally know how to laugh, have fun, and enjoy life. On our way to adulthood, we lose the ability to be happy. Instead, we start hunting for happiness. This is where our trouble starts.

One of my favorite Henry David Thoreau quotes sums up our dilemma: "Happiness is like a butterfly, the more you chase it, the more it will elude you, but if you notice other things around you, it will gently come and sit on your shoulder."

When we actively seek out happiness, we fail. Happiness doesn't come from pursuing wealth, health, or influence. The only way to find joy is to stop focusing so much on ourselves and, instead, live life. Between the pressures of work and the constant social media doom scrolling, you don't need to be reminded that you will die. You need to remember how to live.

What does it mean to live? To borrow a phrase from the insightful Marie Kondo, it means doing the things that spark joy. It also means learning to find joy in the things you have to do.

To paraphrase Kondo again, does money spark joy? The data shows that money only buys you happiness up to a point. This is the place where many people get lost. We want to hoard money because it is useful for buying things like food, shelter, and security. We need those things to be happy. But we are poor judges of when we have enough. Some part of our brains always wants more money, and then we start spending on status symbols. How do we get more money? We trade little bits of our lives for it.

You work extra hours at the office, or you start another side hustle. You want a little bit more money. You know that if you could make six figures or seven figures, you'd be happy. But your time is limited. When you trade your time away to your boss or your business, you are shrinking the amount of life you have to enjoy.

Does your work spark joy? Does making more money make you happier than walking in the park with your family? Self-help doesn't work because it draws our attention inside of ourselves when the greatest sources of happiness are outside of ourselves.

The greatest sources of joy are creativity, friends, family, and community. Each of these things requires us to put our focus outside of ourselves. When you create something, whether it be music, art, crafts, food, or anything else, you tap into a powerful place that is otherwise inaccessible. The true magic happens when you share your creativity. When you use your skills and love to make someone else's day a little brighter, you feel happier.

You also feel happy when you are with the people you love. Think about how you feel when you hug the people you love. Remember how happy you were the last time your child, partner, or parent received good news. The bonds that bind us also spark joy. There is no to-do list or side hustle that can generate the same positive vibes as playing in the yard with your children and a new puppy.

Joy can also be found beyond our inner circle of friends and family. Happiness comes from serving your community. When you give your time and resources to someone else, without the expectation of reward, you will find happiness waiting for you. When it comes to service, the key is giving of your time. Cutting a check may be important, but the tax-deductible charity will not provide you the same happiness return as spending time directly with people in your community.

This doesn't mean that you should never look inside yourself. Living a happy life is like driving a car. You need to glance inside at the dashboard from time to time. It's helpful to monitor your speed, to see how much fuel you have left, and to watch for any warning lights. However, if you spend more time looking inside at the dashboard than you do looking out through your car's windshield, you're going to crash.

When you start each day by asking, "How can I live today?" you will begin to see everything shift in your life. That doesn't mean it's a magic incantation. You still have to make changes in the way you live. You have to decide to prioritize things that spark joy. There is nothing more frightening than standing at a decision point and choosing to do something that sparks joy instead of something more conventional that your people will understand.

After years of being a successful freelance writer, my people still shake their heads at my decision to forego getting a "real" job. They wonder how I can live with all that uncertainty. However, they also acknowledge that I'm happier and more pleasant to be around than I was before. I have also made a conscious decision not to maximize my income.

I forego a lot of money-making opportunities because I have enough. That doesn't mean I don't want to grow my business. I am not opposed to earning more money. But I have chosen to stop chasing it. I am chasing experiences that make me feel alive. If more money comes my way while I'm living life, so much the better. I'm also content with where I'm at. Often, I still chase things that don't matter. That's when I turn to my memento vitae.

SCHOOLCHILDREN'S EYES FIND

HEART IN A HORSE CHESTNUT HALF

A SMALL FALL TREASURE

It's a chestnut half that my daughter found on the ground while we walked down the hill from school five years ago. She was eight years old and having a tough time adjusting to a new school. She picked it up off the ground and gave it to me.

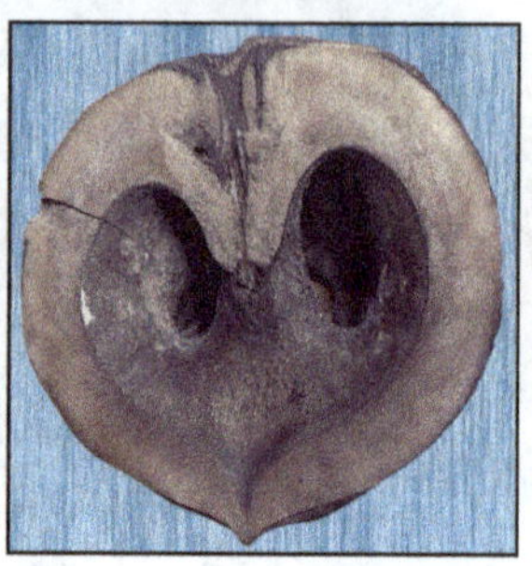

"Look!" she said. "It has a heart inside! It's like a valentine. I want you to keep it, Daddy."

This chestnut half sits on my desk just below my monitor. When I look at it, I remember my daughter's love and enthusiasm. I recognize the importance of looking around at my surroundings because you never know what treasures you may find. And, I remember that there is more to life than work, side hustles, and to-do lists.

The chestnut half with the heart in the middle reminds me to live life. Living our lives and helping others is the only way to find the joy that eludes our most dogged pursuits. The next time you feel like something is missing in your life, ask yourself, "How can I live today?"

Then go and do that thing.

Chapter 7

How to Find the Extraordinary Hidden in your Everyday Life

I have never seen this sunset before.

This is the thought that bursts into my mind with such explosive force that it momentarily mutes all the thoughts, voices, and conversations that are otherwise always bouncing around in my brain; like when a server drops a tray of dishes in a restaurant and in the moments after the echoes of the crashing and smashing have faded; all conversations remain in suspended animation a beat longer.

I'm standing on Lincoln Beach in Oregon on a windy, crisp, and unusually clear fall day at low tide, partaking in my most sacred beach ritual, the sunset walk. I'm about a half mile away from the Fishing Rock State Park, a bluff that juts into the Pacific, which happens to be the perfect place to watch a sunset or to spot migrating humpback whales.

The wind is tugging at my hood, stinging my cheeks with cold salt water and sand; sea tears.

Geologically speaking, the North Oregon coast is much younger than beaches in Southern California or Florida. The sand is coarser, closer to the rocky outcrops that still dot the coast here than the smooth sand that has been beaten and refined by the relentless ocean in those warmer locales. I'm wearing my water socks, waterproof shoes with rubber soles that protect me against sharp rocks and coarse sand, but not the bitter cold of the water.

I head north, towards what our family calls "the cliffs," fixing Fishing Rock in my sights, putting the ocean and sunset to my right shoulder.

It hits me again.

I've never seen this sunset before.

I realize that this thought is neither novel nor profound. Of course I have never lived today before. Of course each day, and everything it contains, is a new experience. A twist on a trope, a variation on a theme.

I remember staying here with my family and some of our friends a few winters ago. It was a clear day then, too. All of us went out on the deck of the beach house to watch the sunset. After less than a minute, the son-in-law, married to their oldest daughter, proclaimed, with an arrogance peculiar to young men, that he was going inside because he'd already seen plenty of sunsets.

That connects me to a line from the movie *Moneyball*, adapted from the book of the same name by Michael Lewis, about my beloved, and now relocated, Oakland A's. Brad Pitt's character, Billy Beane, finishes watching a film of a minor league baseball game that shows a heartwarming tale and says, "How can you not be romantic about baseball?"

How can you not be romantic about sunsets?

I've never seen this sunset before.

Partly to keep the wind out of my eyes and partly out of a deep-rooted, crow-like compulsion, I keep my head down and scan the sand as I walk, searching for agates, shells, or other beach treasures. I keep the ocean in my peripheral view, as sneaker waves, even at low tide, have the potential to knock over the unwary.

I catch sight of a possible agate near a retreating wave and dash to grab it before it disappears below the sand. It's not an agate this time, but a smooth piece of polished shell. In our family, we call these shell bits shark teeth because I used to tell the kids that's what they were. The sea brings out the liar in me. This one has curves and looks like a tiny pale model of a southwestern desert hoodoo. I pocket it.

Back home, back where my family is enjoying the warmth that a house and furnace provide in late autumn, we have a large jar full of agates and shark teeth. Whenever one of us goes to the coast, we bring back one or two offerings for the jar. Nobody else knows this, but that jar is my favorite thing our family has. I love it even more than all the wonderful pictures that are spread out over the walls in our hall of frame, or even more than the paintings I inherited from my grandma.

From a distance, it looks like a big, plain glass container filled with bits of white rock. But when you get up close, you can see the different textures, sizes, and shades. There are amber agates and countless shades of white shells and sea stones. Each thing in the jar is one-of-a-kind. All are shaped by the same or similar processes between the ocean and sand, but each is shaped by unique circumstances.

Each agate, each shell fragment, has a history. Each one has arrived in that jar through a series of statistically unlikely events so improbable that the existence of everything in that jar is an individual miracle. I stop and face the ocean.

The sun is at the beginning of its melting phase in its nightly performance. Like a magic trick, each evening, the fireball in the sky melts as it hits the horizon, scattering across the water until it disappears.

I have never seen this sunset before.

God, how can you not be romantic about sunsets? Distracted by the show, a frigid, ankle-deep wave hits me and pulls me back into the present. Nobody hears me cackle with the joy of being right here in this moment, alone but not lonely.

I'm near the bluff now. It's decision time. Do I walk up to get the elevated view and miss a few minutes of the sunset, or do I stay on the beach and soak up every last shard of sunshine? Faux shark teeth are nice, but an agate is the real prize.

I stay on the beach and turn south so the sunset is on my left shoulder, and the wind pushes my hood further on my head instead of trying to rip it off. I keep scanning for agates while also keeping track of the sun and the ocean.

The sun is most of the way gone now. It looks like a puddle of radioactive ooze on the horizon. The sky is still in the middle of its transformation. The blue darkened at its highest reaches, and has become a watercolor mixture of red and purple near the horizon.

I spot another potential treasure and scramble to grab it before the incoming wave pulls it back into the ocean. This time, it is an agate. This one is a translucent light amber, forged in some underwater volcano millions of years ago and just now surfacing on the beach I happen to be combing. A miracle just for me.

I pocket the agate and stare at the disappearing sun. This same celestial body I couldn't bear to look at a few hours ago without risking permanent injury, I can now gaze on fondly as the Pacific swallows its last sliver.

The red sky puts in my mind both an old saying from my grandma and the closing lines of the 1963 Cary Grant and Audrey Hepburn film, *Charade*. Grant's character reassures Hepburn's character that the red sunset is a good omen and repeats the old rhyme, "Red sky at night, a sailor's delight. Red sky in morning, the sailor takes warning."

I will head home tomorrow. But at least the weather will be good. That is when I have another thought that, while not profound, reframes everything in my life. This is the last and only time I will ever see this sunset.

While I have seen plenty of sunsets, and if fate will have it, I will yet see even more sunsets in the future, this sunset before me right now is a once-in-a-lifetime event, never seen before and never to be seen again. Not in human history. Not in geological history. Not in the past or future of the universe. Only right here and right now.

I'm standing on the edge of the continent, witnessing the inexorable results of geology, physics, and cosmology in the world that I am a part of. Sunsets may happen every day, but each sunset is singular, an impossible-to-duplicate event, and here I am watching this one from open to close.

Sunsets like tears, snowflakes, agates, and grains of sand can either be seen as ordinary, everyday occurrences, or if you're daring, can be seen as the culmination of a myriad of complex processes, producing an almost impossibly unique miracle that you are fortunate to be a part of.

I have never seen this sunset before. This is the last and only time I will ever see this sunset.

How can you not be romantic about sunsets?

SAILORS
AND
LOVERS

ARE UNIVERSE'S
GREATEST
FOOLS

MAKE ME
TWICE THE
FOOL

Chapter 8

The Joy of Nothing

Throughout my accidental career as a poet-cartoonist, I've explored lots of unlikely themes. I've written about everything from pirate love letters to the end of the Anthropocene. But when I look back at the thousands of poems I've written and the hundreds of comics I've made, one theme keeps surfacing.

Nothing.

Nothing allows me to live in the moment, and it's the pure essence of mindfulness. Blank agendas, empty canvases, and resisting the urge to hustle all strengthen the bonds of love and grease the wheels of creativity.

I'm so committed to the joy of nothing that I've used that exact line in two different haiku comics, and it pops up ridiculously often in my drafts.

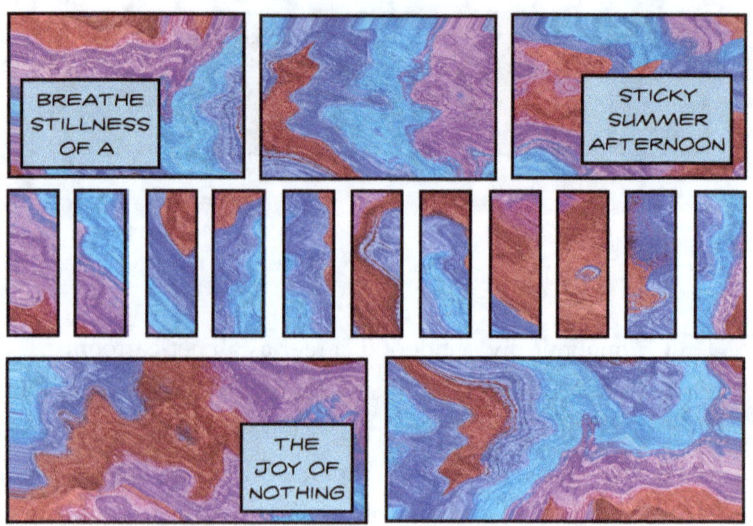

This isn't even the first essay I've started called "The Joy of Nothing."

Because we live in a world where everything is just a click away, learning to sit with nothing is more important than ever. This is especially true if you want to live a life of creativity. Doing nothing is not about being lazy. It's an act of resistance in a society where every move is monitored, every message is about increasing productivity, and every second is filled with noise disguised as information.

Nothing is the space where love finds us. It's the place where our intuition whispers to us. Nothing is where we are most alive.

MINDLESSLY DRIVING
ON WINDY SCENIC BACKROADS
THE JOY OF NOTHING

Most people are too scared of their thoughts to be comfortable with doing nothing for long stretches. Doing nothing is difficult. It takes discipline to turn off your phone and let your mind wander where it will until it empties of thought and worry. But the rewards are incredible.

At its heart, the philosophy of Taoism is about holding space for nothing. When you allow the stream of life to carry you in its currents, you always arrive precisely where you need to be. One of the great struggles of my life has been to embrace nothing. Because of childhood trauma, I became an ambitious, productivity-obsessed doer of big things as an adult. This made me miserable.

It wasn't until I suffered a nervous breakdown and lost everything I had professionally worked to build that I began to submit to nothing. Nothing is not depression. I've been there as well, and while depression is a hopeless void, nothing is a joyful, open-ended canvas. With nothing, there is no regret or anxiety, for those require your mind to be trapped in the past or the future. Nothing is only now.

I have a daily nothing practice. I walk outside, in nature if possible, without any agenda for as long as possible. I don't track my steps, I don't set an intention, I simply exist. I walk and notice what's around me. My mind usually races for the first twenty minutes or so, trying to solve business problems or art problems. Then it settles down, and I'm left with thoughts of my footsteps, the squirrels scampering along the oak tree branches overhead, and nothing else.

After my nothing time, I often write haiku about what I have seen, doing my best to stay a few more moments in the present, in the warm embrace of nothing. After these long walks, I'm always happier and lighter. More often than not, my mind shows me simple ways to navigate through or around obstacles that previously seemed impassable as I drive back home from a walk.

This past year, life has been more difficult for me than usual.

I've had several business setbacks, and several of my family members have had serious health challenges that required a lot of my time and focus because I am the primary caregiver in our family.

Early this fall, when everyone was back to full health, I realized I was exhausted. I had nothing physically, mentally, or emotionally to give anyone. I was teetering on burnout. I needed an extended time to do nothing because I have learned that actively doing nothing is how I heal my soul.

It's critical to note what doing nothing does not include. Doing nothing does not include scrolling social media or doing anything on your phone. Doing nothing is not the same as lying on the couch and binge-watching your comfort show. Nothing may require you to experience boredom.

I decided to travel across the country to Daytona Beach for reasons I did not understand then. I spent three days sleeping late and walking up and down the beach. When I was hungry, I ate, but otherwise, I did nothing but walk the beach and swim in the ocean.

I didn't write anything. I didn't draw anything. I didn't make any plans. I emptied my mind and filled my senses with the sights, sounds, smells, tastes, and textures of the world around me. I now understand it was a kind of pilgrimage.

Those days on the beach were a sacred experience that I'm still processing months later and that I'm reluctant to write about in too much detail lest I profane the gift the universe gave me. I returned home a different person, filled with more joy for life than I have had in a very long time.

Had I decided to spend my entire trip doing touristy stuff or visiting as many theme parks as possible, I would've returned entertained and maybe even happy. But I would not have had the transcendental experience that can only come by not seeking one. Nothing was the most important thing I could've done then, and I still feel the effects of that nothing in my daily life.

Life is not perfect, but it never has been. Still, I wake up excited for each day, and no matter what is happening in the world or my life, I have the presence to find small pockets of wonder. I know this will not last forever.

Every day, you and I are assaulted with requests for our attention from people who do not mean us well. The only way to escape these demands is to not engage; to actively choose to do nothing as often as possible.

When was the last time you experienced the joy of nothing?

Chapter 9

The Night Sky is a Landscape of Hope

Whether I die instantly in a supernova or perish from a slow exhaustion of all of my fuel, I hope that, like the stars, everything that is most precious inside of me will illuminate the darkest moments of my descendants' lives as they fix their course and navigate uncharted waters.

Of all the things we can least afford to have a scarcity of in our world right now, hope is at the top of the list. There has never been a revolution, scientific breakthrough, or solution to a society-threatening problem discovered without hope.

Hope is a unique virtue that requires you to live and work in the present to build a better future, understanding all of the problems you face in the present moment. Hope is something you must cultivate and maintain. While some of us are more predisposed to holding onto hope, without work, hope will either dissipate or become corrupted into a sense of complacency.

How do you build hope? Hope is made of three ingredients: gratitude, imagination, and wonder. When I start to feel my natural cynicism taking control, I know I must counter that by recharging my sense of gratitude, imagination, and wonder.

The easiest way for me to do that is to walk in the dark, under the stunning night sky. The night sky is a landscape of hope.

The stars are impossibly ancient and inconceivably far away. The night sky unites all of us Earthlings. It allows us to look up and see that there is more to our universe than our small planet. The stars connect us to the past and the future. The light we see from the stars has traveled so far that their sources may no longer even exist. Their light still shines for us, inspiring us to reach beyond our current limitations.

When walking under the stars, I can't help but be awestruck. I soak in the wonders pouring down on me from the heavens. How can you be anything but gobsmacked and grateful when you start to consider how immense the cosmic scale is that our tiny planet is a trifling part of? Somehow, the stars make all of my problems seem manageable.

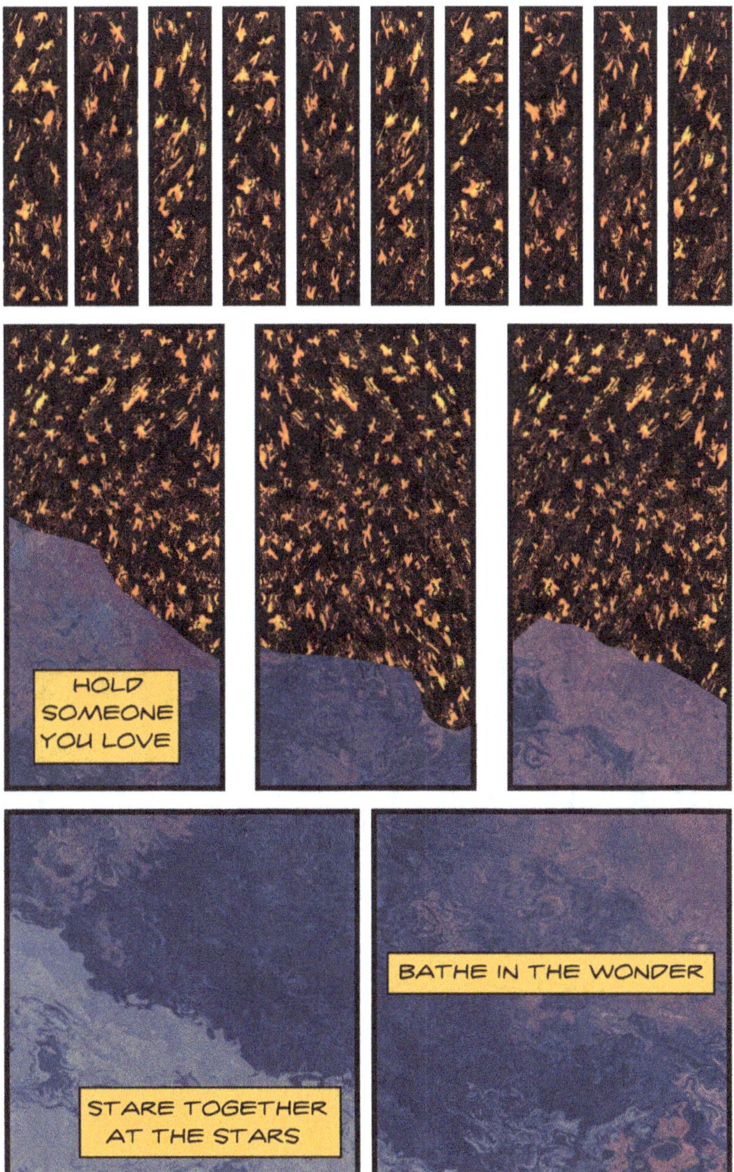
HOLD SOMEONE YOU LOVE
STARE TOGETHER AT THE STARS
BATHE IN THE WONDER

I can start to imagine a way forward, and more importantly, I once again feel the desire to keep trying, sparking inside my soul. While I love to walk alone, I also find that night walks are best with others. Gawking up at the moon and the stars draws you closer and allows you to share secrets you might otherwise keep bottled up.

The night sky cures me of all of my future-gazing tendencies. I forget my anxieties and my regrets. I can only exist in the present under the burden of millions and billions of years of creation beaming down on me as I walk the only place we have found in the whole of the universe that supports such a myriad of life forms we take for granted.

What else could I want from life but the ability to walk, see, and hear the sounds of the heavens? Consumerism seems especially petty in the light of the full moon.

The night sky both allows my imagination to soar and grounds me in my body. I remember that all I am promised is this moment. There is a Buddhist teaching that you have no right to the fruits of your labor. The idea is that you cannot be working, expecting to receive something in the future. Instead, the work of the present moment must be enough for you.

To me, this is the core of hope. I will not see the future fruits from the seeds I plant today. However, I keep planting seeds because I hope the trees will bring shade and delicious sustenance to those who come after me.

I only write and draw because I cannot do anything else, and I hope my art will make a difference to someone else when they stumble upon it. But I have no right to expect anything else from this work.

Even though I am a work-from-home dad, I feel like a lost pilgrim searching the landscapes for clues about the meaning of life. Every time I read a poem by Mary Oliver or an essay from Henry David Thoreau, I am more convinced that whatever I am seeking is in nature.

When strolling under the stars, I feel I am closest to creation, to whatever mysterious force it is that has allowed me to exist. I sense that this force of creation doesn't need or want to be worshipped. It only wants to make me whole and for me to see It inside of me.

The more I see of nature, the more I understand that we are all connected: the trees, the stars, the crabs, and you and I are all parts of the same whole. All of our yearnings are simply different manifestations of the desire to feel that wholeness.

Our brokenness and isolation from the universe cause all of our anger and angst.

This all seems easy to understand when looking up at the night sky, an intuitive truth. When I stop looking up at the stars and the moon, I remember that I live in a dangerous time.

The danger is much less for me than for so many others. But when I glance back upwards, I feel like the sky is chastening me.

The stars seem to whisper, "Have you so quickly forgotten your lessons? You and I are not separate. We have no answers that you do not have inscribed on your soul."

We humans often stretch ourselves thin trying to live in the past, future, and present. We spend so much time worrying about what will happen or about what we have or haven't done before that we have no energy left for the only thing within our control: the present.

Mindfulness is not about productivity.

The goal is not to relax enough to get more done. The point of mindfulness is to continually rediscover that we only exist in this moment. We can only do the work right now.

Hope allows us to have the resolve to do work we will never see the end of.

WE SEARCH
THE HEAVENS
FOR ANSWERS
HIDING WITHIN
THE WALLS OF
OUR HEARTS

The universe has been kind enough to provide us with a night sky filled with wonders so that we can glance into eternity every once in a while and remember how to live in the now.

Chapter 10

Greet Yourself with Kindness

When the sun has been put to bed at the end of another day, do you hold a memorial service or a celebration? What did today mean? I'm an absurdist at heart. I believe that the only inherent meaning in this life is the meaning we choose to make. Since my life will pass no matter what I decide to do with it, I choose each day to create meaning through gentleness, kindness, and creativity.

In the cycles of the sun and the moon, I choose to see a celestial drama that mirrors the cycles in my life. The dawn is a sacred gift; a new birth. It signifies the start of a day whose entire purpose and contents are determined by my actions.

The sunset and the moonrise signal the end of a ritual sacrifice to the gods. A piece of my life has been offered up. Was it a worthy sacrifice? One willing given? Or was it a reluctant offering? One I was compelled to part with despite my desire to hold onto that sliver of life just a little longer?

You and I have a set number of days. Neither you nor I know how many of those days we are allotted. Today is probably not my last day, but it could be. You will, in all likelihood, greet the dawn tomorrow, but that is not guaranteed.

If the stoics are right that the way you do one thing is the way you do everything, then the way you move through today is the way you move through every day. I don't care how much money you made today. I do not care how productive you were or how clever you were. In the end, what does that matter or mean? After your final sunset, you will move on without your money. On the first day you don't wake up, will you care about a clever retort or a missing report?

Each day, you choose what your life will mean. You can greet yourself and others with kindness, cruelty, or indifference. You can perform your duties with conscientious joy, distracted apathy, or angry insolence. The sun will rise and set regardless. These choices matter. These small choices are the difference between a day worthy of a sacred sacrifice and a day that has been desecrated.

Each day, you either consecrate that moment of your life to a noble purpose or you desecrate it. Once the day has passed, you cannot bring it back. You can only decide again tomorrow how you will prepare that sacrifice of twenty-four hours.

Your noble purpose doesn't need to be religious or even spiritual. I write of gods and the universe as higher powers, even though I am not sure there is anything higher than the forces of nature. I choose to notice the wonderful details of the world and ascribe them to a higher order so that I can uplift my state of mind. When I attune myself to the beauty of the dawn and dusk, I find it easier to return my grocery cart to the stall so that the worker will not have to chase it down in the cold and rain. When I find joy in the birds on my lawn each morning, I find it easier to be patient with my children as we scramble to get them to school on time.

Each day is filled with routines of things we would rather not do. What if instead of allowing dread to well up at the thought of hours spent cooking and cleaning, sitting at a desk, standing behind a cash register, or working in the elements, you approached each mundane task as part of a ritual? A routine is a series of thoughtless actions. When you move through the day guided only by habit and muscle memory, you are not living life. You are an automaton—a fleshy robot distinguishable from artificial intelligence only by your need to breathe, eat, and drink.

A ritual is an intentional act. When I wash the dishes as part of my routine, my mind fills with complaints and anxieties. Why can't she at least rinse her dishes? When will he learn not to use so much damn syrup? Will I have time today to finish that chapter that's already a week late?

When I make washing the dishes a ritual, my mind stays in the present and fills with observation and gratitude. How fortunate are we to have enough food to eat? I remember when he was learning to feed himself and kept missing his mouth with the spoon, wailing with frustration each time he struck his cheek. Now, he helps me around the house, and soon, he will leave our home. Washing these dishes so they can be used again is how I care for my family. Washing these dishes so they can be used again, like the sun sets so it can rise tomorrow. Turning your daily responsibilities into rituals that hold meaning for you is an act of tenderness for yourself and for those you love.

When you notice what you are filling your day with, you will start to see for the first time. Before you stumbled through your days with your senses blunted. But once you notice the way you sigh right before a Zoom meeting or how you squint your eyes when you see a message from that one person, you will realize life has been happening without you. Once you notice what you notice, you can shift your attention and intention. I feel lighter when my office blinds are open, and I can see the rain as it falls and strikes the window. I can choose to greet everyone in the next meeting with genuine affection. I can be excited to see them as people who also have loves and pains, and not just as co-workers.

Just as I once witnessed the mosque bells call the people to prayer in the Muslim Quarter in Xian, the sunset summons me daily to my most sacred ritual. No matter where I am or what I am doing, I always take the time to note that the sun is setting. I may not always be able to watch the sunset, but I can always notice when it is happening. And in that moment of noticing, I perform my ritual.

I ask, was today a worthy sacrifice? If I can answer yes, my whole body warms, and light shoots from my eyes. If I must answer no, I then forgive myself and tell myself, tomorrow I have another opportunity. Once I accept the forgiveness, my whole body warms up, and light shoots from my eyes.

I do not need a priest, mediator, or guide between me and nature, between me and forgiveness, between me and the feeling of being me.

When you choose to make your own meaning in life, when you stop and notice the birds on the lawn or the leaves in the air, when you stop sleepwalking through each day, it is then that you can greet yourself with the kindness and tenderness you crave, that you deserve. Only once you learn to meet yourself in this way are you prepared to greet those who are closest to you with that same kindness and tenderness.

Once you begin to truly notice those closest to you, you will start to see others, acquaintances, co-workers, and even strangers, as who they truly are: pilgrims stranded on this rock, moving through the vastness of space, seeking the chance to be seen for who they truly are.

As different as we all are, all of us are headed for the same destination. When the sun has been put to bed at the end of another day, do you hold a memorial service or a celebration? I choose to celebrate.

I am not perfect. I'm still prone to complaining about petty grievances. But when I notice that I have slipped out of the magic of my rituals and back into the mundane routines of a former life, I greet myself with tenderness. I do not berate myself or even chide myself. I just laugh and begin a new ritual cycle.

Each day, you choose how you will live your life and how you will move through the world. I hope you will use your power of attention to notice what you are truly doing each day and to then greet yourself with kindness. The simple act of treating yourself with tenderness and kindness will not only change you—it will change your world.

Chapter 11

A Season of Rest and Celebration

One of the strangest compliments managers give is calling someone who produces a lot of work a "machine." Why would any human being want to be a machine? Machines work until they break, and then they're replaced. But so many employers and hustle-and-grind-until-you-die influencers sell you on this idea that success only comes to those who outwork everyone else.

As a society, we put the most pressure to work like, and even look like, a machine on women. From mothers being expected to work a full-time job to help make ends meet and to then work a second shift once they get home, taking care of the children, and often their male partners, to our impossible beauty standards that treat any woman over 25 as an old hag, the message is clear: work until you break. Olivia Rodrigo sums it up perfectly in her song *all-american bitch* when she says she's built like a mother and a total machine.

One of the fundamentals of our humanity is the need for rest. As the code bros are fond of saying, this is a feature, not a bug. Rest is when our body and mind heal from the rigors of life. It's also when all the information we have taken in is synthesized. If you care about creativity, you need to have periods of idleness. You need to do what farmers used to do to their fields in the time before corporate agricultural conglomerates. You need to lie fallow.

We talk and act as if human beings are separate from nature. But we are a part of nature, and as such, we are subject to the seasons, just like the birds, trees, and squirrels. You need a season of rest, and because humans are a communal species, you also need a season of celebration.

We often treat winter like it is our enemy. In Shakespeare's sonnets and plays, the winter of life is the time to prepare to die. Winter is a time of healing and renewal.

One sign that a tree is unhealthy is that it keeps its leaves longer in winter than other trees. Fifteen years ago, I planted four apple trees, two pear trees, and two plum trees in our backyard. At the time, I knew nothing about trees or growing fruit. Over the past fifteen years, I've learned through books, observation, and hard work how to care for my trees. One thing I've noticed year-after-year is that the trees that have the healthiest blooms in the spring are the ones that shed their leaves the earliest in the fall. In turn, the healthiest blooms become the best apples, pears, or plums.

When one of my apple trees never shed half of its leaves in the fall and winter, it also failed to bloom in spring. It produced no fruit because it had a fungal infection that took me three years to cure fully. The failure to let go is a sign of disease, not strength.

We have been conditioned to think about work from the moment we wake up until the seconds before we fall into a restless sleep, haunted by alerts and notifications from our phones. Again, the failure to let go is a sign of disease, not strength.

For the past twelve-and-a-half years, I've worked as a solo creative business owner. I'm a freelance writer and illustrator, as well as a poet-cartoonist. Over that span, I've come to understand that I'm not so different from my trees. There are seasons to my creative life. I cannot make things all the time. That leads to burnout and me not making anything for long periods of time.

I need time to rest. Time to do nothing but celebrate the fruits of my labor and ready myself for another round of making things. I need the winter.

I use the winter season here in the Pacific Northwest to slow down. For my entire adult life, I have always taken the last week or two of the year off. I don't meet with clients, I don't submit to editors, and I don't stress about getting things done.

I cannot do this all winter, of course, but for the months of December, January, and February, I go partially dormant. During this time, I let the ideas I've encountered throughout the year ferment into some new concoctions. When spring comes, I'm bursting with new ideas for projects.

I find a particular beauty and peace in the quiet stillness of winter. Maybe this is because I'm getting older, or maybe it's because I'm finally learning to love myself enough to see that I have value as a human being beyond what I can produce. My work for clients and myself is much richer, and it connects with others in a much deeper way when I have time to let my brain and body quasi-hibernate.

Your seasons will be different from mine. If you have an employer, you will have more obstacles to adjusting your work cycle throughout the year. However, I have found that for most people, the real obstacle to having a season of rest and celebration is their self-loathing.

The poet Mary Oliver explains in her poem *Wild Geese* that you don't have to be good. You are enough. You don't have to earn rest through PTO or some other corporate nonsense. Rest is your right as a human, as a beast of nature. You must claim it. But do not delude yourself by thinking you must first be worthy of rest.

You are you. You are human. You are enough. You are worthy.

Winter is a time for cozy thoughts. It's a time to be soft and slow. Now, I look forward to the winter because it means I have made it another year.

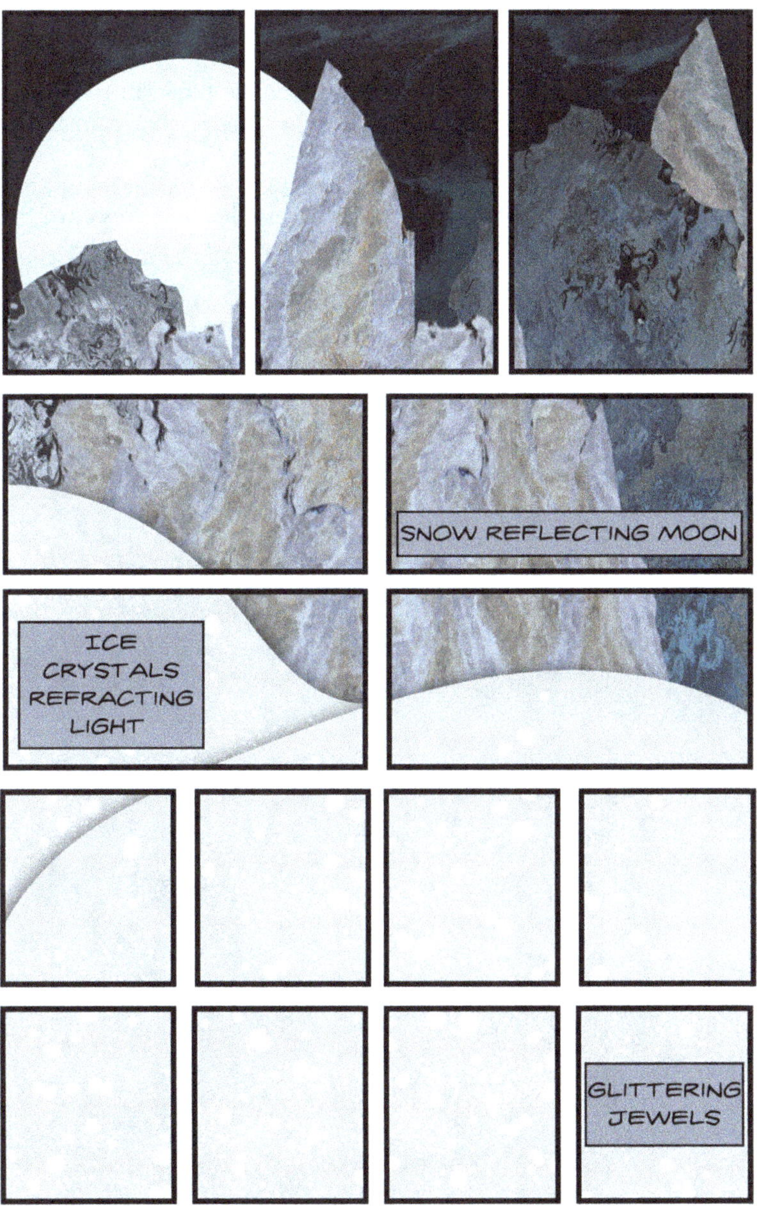
SNOW REFLECTING MOON
ICE CRYSTALS REFRACTING LIGHT
GLITTERING JEWELS

Do my slow seasons affect my income? I'm sure they do. But I make enough to allow me and my family to live comfortably by planning for the slow season all year. The memories we make in the winter are far more valuable to me than a few extra gigs or publication credits.

Right now, my apple trees are bare, and piles of leaves cover the ground below them. Their branches extend towards the sky, asking the winter to come. I join them in greeting the cold winter, my season of rest and celebration. I hope you will join the trees and me in our season of being soft and slow.

Chapter 12

How to Get Through the Hard Stuff

Grit is important. I get it—you get it—we all get it! But why is most advice about how to build grit so awful and so vague?

Grit, sometimes known as resilience in more clinical places, is the ability to keep your life moving forward after setbacks. While it is a universal truth that no human life is without pain or problems, it often feels like so many people who choose to write about grit have never faced a setback in life that they didn't have enough money to handle.

Better planning doesn't solve poverty. Happy mantras cannot dispel years of abuse. Smiling won't bring back loved ones who have passed on.

And while all pain is relative, the truth is that coming from a certain level of wealth protects you against the worst elements of the tragedies and traumas that most of us have to live through. So much advice about resilience comes down to the simple lines from the wonderful children's book, *We're Going on a Bear Hunt*, "We can't go over it. We can't go under it. Oh no! We've got to go through it!"

Telling this to an adult as a way of saying you should have grit is a bit like telling someone who is drowning that their life would be better if they would just keep their head above the water. You already know you have to go through this dark period. You need the strength to get back up and a reason to keep trying. I don't know what you're going through. But I do know what I have gone through. At the risk of sounding like a contestant in the Trauma Olympics, here are some of the challenges I've faced:

- Physical abuse at the hands of a parent
- Emotional abuse at the hands of a parent
- Religious trauma
- Cancer
- Mental health struggles
- Adult ADHD
- Loss of a career
- Financial collapse and bankruptcy
- Dealing with the welfare system
- Suicidal ideation
- Addiction in close family members
- Untimely deaths of parents and other family members
- Chronic illnesses in my children and spouse

I share these challenges not to boast or to generate pity. I want you to know that I have been through some shit. Many of these challenges have happened concurrently or in close succession. Your life may be infinitely harder than what I have gone through. I consider myself to be fortunate. I love my life, and while that has not always been the case, I do recognize that I have a lot of privilege because of my race, gender, and sexual identity.

Life is not a competition to see who has had it worse, but I also believe it's easier to hear someone talk about grit who has suffered and who didn't have a reservoir of cash to cushion the blow. At the darkest times in my life, I had to stay home and face things, not head off to three different countries on two continents to find myself again.

How do you find the strength to keep going while lying at the bottom of a ravine? How do you find a reason to keep moving forward when everything you know has been taken from you?

There is not one right answer. The exact recipe that will work for you is different from what has worked for me. But there are two things everyone who has to go through hard things must find. You must find small pockets of joy in your life, and you must find a way to name and face your emotions. One of the great superpowers that every human has is the ability to see what they are looking for. If you set your mind to find small things that are good in your life, no matter how awful a state you are in, you will find them.

These small pockets of joy will not solve your problems or magically carry you through to the other side of your grief or trauma. However, these brief moments of gratitude or pockets of joy do act as small places of refuge as you work your way through your troubles. Think of them as tiny oases in the desert. You stop at one oasis to rest and replenish your supplies before heading out again, where you will look for another oasis where you can stop. One of the ways I found small pockets of joy was by writing haiku about the world around me. I would take long walks and write small poems about what I saw. Other times, I would sit at a window and write haiku about what I noticed happening outside.

These short, three-line poems became my meditation. They turned into a mindfulness exercise. Later, I would learn to go deeper with this practice by creating haiku comics. These short illustrations made me focus more intensely on simple daily events like sunsets and gave me something to look forward to.

Other people find this same kind of relief from the struggles of life through sketchbooks, traditional meditation, walks through the city or nature, and journaling. The key is to notice what you notice.

During one particularly rough stretch for my family, I found daily joy in taking my children to school. I created a playlist for the car that had specific songs that each individual child loved. We sang and laughed as we drove to school, easing their anxiety about the new schools they were attending and filling me with a sense of happiness at seeing their temporary relief from the dread they were carrying around due to the circumstances of our lives.

I noticed that I found joy in trying to bring joy to my children. Over time, I came to understand that part of my problem was my wallowing in my problems, and that part of the way out of the dilemma I was facing was to focus on helping others.

I stumbled upon an ancient notion that a good life was not based on wealth but on human connection. Searching for small joys became a habit and then a discipline that allowed me to let go of my painful past and release my expectations for the future. All that was left was to live in the present.

All of that transformation happened over a period of many years. But, at the moment, in the day-to-day of navigating poverty and difficult family dynamics, searching for small pockets of joy helped me survive one hour at a time on days when I wasn't sure I could even take life one day at a time.

If life is overwhelming, stop trying to solve everything and just look for one tiny thing that makes you smile. That can be enough for right now. When you string enough of these small pockets of joy together, you find the strength to get back up after life has sucker punched you and left you in a heap by the side of the road.

You cannot reason your way out of grief, shame, or any of the other difficult human emotions that often trap us. The only way to get relief from these feelings is to name and face them. You have to discover what it is you are feeling. Because of my upbringing, I did not know how to identify hardly any of my feelings until well into middle age. This is still something I struggle with.

However, I am a master at suppressing uncomfortable feelings. At different times in my life, years of suppressed emotions have exploded out of me, leaving me bewildered and floundering. For most of my life, I thought of myself as being pretty chill. I rarely ever got angry, and I didn't hold grudges. Then I had the rug pulled out from underneath me in my mid-thirties, and everything made me mad. I knew I was filled with rage, but I had no idea what to do about it. I knew I didn't want to yell at my kids the way my father had yelled at me. But sometimes, it felt like the rage just spilled out of me, often without any provocation.

That was when I started doing something that sounded crazy. On days when my rage felt all-consuming, I would get into my car, drive to Walmart, park in the far corner of the lot, and scream as loud as I could. The first time I did this, I felt such relief that I cried for ten minutes.

Yelling in my car became something I did at least once a week, and this practice led to two surprising outcomes. One, it meant I never yelled anywhere else. I wasn't traumatizing my children with my anger. Two, I started to yell about what I was feeling, and I discovered I was carrying anger and shame about things that had happened to me as a child that I had never dealt with. I had just taken those emotions and stuffed them as far down as possible.

I had never understood that I had felt shame, but with the help of therapy and my own study, I came to learn that my shame was what fueled my anger. This discovery led me to go on a quest to learn more about how I express and feel different emotions. I had no idea that I experienced emotions in my body. I was in my thirties, had an advanced degree, and was still learning how basic human emotions work.

The more I practiced experiencing my emotions, even the negative ones, and identifying those emotions, the better regulated I became. One thing I did to teach myself about my emotions was to create a document I called *How to Become Indomitable*, where I listed all of the things I did to experience emotions. I listed over 130 activities, including everything from crying and laughing to gardening and walking.

One of the great self-help lies is that if you are sad or discouraged, it is your fault for not thinking enough positive thoughts. Life happens to all of us. Often, the greatest hurts we sustain are not our fault at all. However, how we deal with what has happened to us is our responsibility. You do not need to blame yourself to change yourself.

Often, the emotions that feel too much to bear will never fully go away. When you grieve over the death of a loved one, that grief never leaves. It does, however, become more manageable once you submit to feeling that grief.

Understanding the difference between blame and responsibility is empowering. Just like it is not your fault that someone rear-ends you, it is still your responsibility to deal with the insurance fallout and to get your car repaired. The same is true for anything that happens to you in life. You don't need to feel guilt or shame over what happened to take responsibility for identifying and feeling your feelings.

When a wound is fresh, figuring out what you feel may seem impossible. The good news is that you don't need to sort it all out right now. What you need to do is find a way to get to tomorrow.

Some days, this might mean distracting yourself. It might mean creating something ridiculous to look forward to. On my worst days, I would promise myself that if I got through today, I would treat myself to a soda at McDonald's for lunch the next day. I would take my homemade peanut butter and jelly sandwich, go through the drive-thru, order a Large $1 Coke (what I called the "greatest deal in America"), and then feel like a king eating my meager lunch in my car.

Rebuilding your life doesn't mean living a life worthy of a Hollywood Oscar-bait film. Grit just means finding a way to get through today, the next hour, or even the next five minutes. Life is built of moments. When you are going through the hardest times, the fact that you are willing to look for joy and name your emotions means you have grit.

Grit isn't glamorous. Grit often looks like breaking down. It can be screaming in your car, sobbing yourself to sleep, or it can mean cooking breakfast for dinner. The fact that you survive to see another day means you are in the process of "going through it." The only path through the hard parts of life is time. Grit is whatever you need to do to buy yourself more time.

Chapter 13

How to Use Procrastination

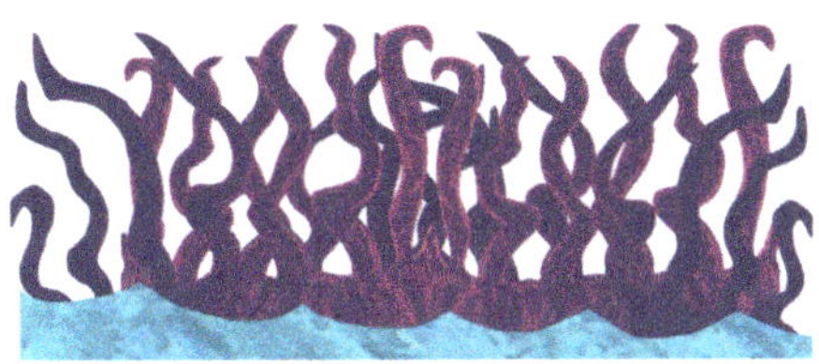

I used to feel like procrastination was a monster that lurked inside of me. It felt completely out of my control. My whole life, I would be doing great, then, without warning, something inside of me would surface and choke my will to be productive. I was told I was self-sabotaging, but procrastination felt like a separate entity with its own will and agenda.

I tried all kinds of tricks to be more productive. I was once high-functioning. I did well in college, went to law school, and graduated in the top third of my class despite my regular bouts of procrastination.

However, I was always getting things done at the very last minute. This increased my stress levels and meant I would throw up each morning before heading off to work at the law firm.

Eventually, I learned that I had an anxiety disorder and ADHD. This seemed to explain the origin of my procrastination, but it did nothing to help me conquer the beast. It wasn't until I decided to study my procrastination like Jane Goodall embedded with a troop of chimpanzees that I understood what was happening.

After leaving the practice of law, I gave myself permission to do things when I felt ready to accomplish them. This had the immediate effect of reducing my anxiety and improving my ability to get things done.

By submitting to procrastination, I took away its power. There was still more to do. I needed to figure out how to deal with my fears that often unleashed the procrastination monster. After reading many books and blog posts and paying attention to what I did while procrastinating, I made a surprising discovery.

The reason I wasn't more productive wasn't that I was procrastinating. Productivity was fake. When it came to the creative work I was doing, procrastination was a feature, not a bug.

Creative work is not quantifiable by the same productivity metrics we use to measure auto parts assembly or data entry. When your job is to make something new, staring off into space might be the best possible use of your time.

Creativity isn't about how many words you wrote today. It's about making sure you write down the right words. You cannot count the number of lines you drew to see if you had a successful art session. You can't even really count the hours spent working on a project to decide whether you were productive.

Does the time in the shower where you came up with the perfect headline count? What about the inspiration that struck you while eating a stale doughnut at an overrated bakery?

PROCRASTINATION

HAS NEVER
KILLED ANYONE

WAIT FOR
TOMORROW

. . .

British advertising genius and author Rory Sutherland explained the role procrastination has in creative work to Rick Rubin on the Tetragrammaton podcast when answering a question about why someone should work in advertising:

> ...This is my plug to why anybody should work there, but it's also my plug for your industry, it's a plug for quite a few other industries, but it's not a plug for becoming an actuary. It's one of those jobs where almost anything you do can make you better at your job. If you are instinctively curious, anything you do, going to the cinema, sitting in a cafe watching the world, buying something, selling something, going to a website, almost anything you can do has the chance of providing you with a useful insight.

Ideas for poems, essays, comics, books, video scripts for clients, and other projects always find me while I'm doing something else. Often, the moment I get in my car after a walk, a haiku pops into my mind. Doodling in my notebook often triggers an idea that launches me into a creative frenzy.

Taking walks in the middle of the day or screwing around on my phone might look like I'm wasting time. However, because I never turn my brain off, because everything I encounter sparks questions, almost everything I do furthers my creative projects.

In other words, procrastinating makes me better at my job. Creative work requires blank canvases. You cannot create meaningful, high-quality work if you never give yourself the time and space to *not* work. Productivity is fundamentally detrimental to creativity. You write incredible sales copy, poetry, or novels by exploring the detours in life.

You aren't ready to do interesting work until you have satisfied your curiosity. When you partner with procrastination and notice what you notice, you will stop feeling anxiety over not getting work done. Instead, you will be excited over the new ideas you draw from your everyday life.

There is one crucial caveat. While you shouldn't be spending eight hours a day staring at a screen, at some point, you must park your butt in a chair and do the actual creative work. Even detours must eventually lead you to a destination.

Many creators fall into the trap of waiting for inspiration when the truth is that inspiration is embedded in daily life. Being open and curious as you go about your day will mean that when it is time to write a client email campaign or your historical fiction novel, you will have something to say.

Procrastination is not a monster lurking inside you, eager to strangle your productivity. It's a guide to your most interesting creative work. Pay attention to what you want to do when you are procrastinating, and you will find the detour you need to follow to have a more fulfilling, creative life. Give yourself the space to notice things.

If you're feeling stuck professionally or creatively, perhaps the way out is to waste more time. It might be the most productive thing you can do.

Chapter 14

Looking for Signs

The most remarkable thing about humans is our ability to find meaning in places where there is none. Whether finding Jesus on a stale sandwich, searching for our fates in the distant lights of the stars, or creating complex interior monologues for our non-verbal pets, being human means discovering stories.

There's a school of thought that we should be rational and move on from our superstitions. These often well-meaning, but often also completely miserable, rationalists want us to see the world for how it really is. Of course, there is mounting evidence that the observable universe is a hologram, so I don't know why rationalists think they know what reality is.

Rationalists have given us economics, a system of flawed predictive models that often fail because of the presumption that humans make rational, self-interested decisions.

Being hyper-rational cuts against our humanity. It's the kind of thing that promotes artificial intelligence. A fellow poet and collaborator recently sent me a link to a story about a study where people preferred AI-generated poetry to human-made poetry. My first indelicate reaction to this was to exclaim out loud to only my phone, "Why the fuck would he send me this?"

I did read the story, and I noticed something. People only preferred AI poetry when they didn't know it was generated by a soulless, climate-killing machine. Poetry is more than an arrangement of words and phrases. It's a human confession. Poetry is seeing Jesus on the toasted bread, hearing the voice of your dead mother in the wind, and longing for a home you've never been to. AI cannot write poetry; it can only arrange words in a way that is statistically-likely to be pleasing to read.

If you are creative, or want to be creative, you need to forget being rational. There is nothing rational about making art or doing any craft. If you want to be rational, be an economist and prepare for a life of dismal gloom. If you want joy, be more human, be irrational. Be an absurdist. Absurdists see the world as lacking any inherent meaning and choose instead to create meaning.

All art is in some way absurd. It is a type of sign-seeking. If you want to be creative, be more human. Look for the stories that aren't there and discover meaning in the meaningless. Art is about truth—not scientific truth—but human truth. We need scientific truth in this world. I want vaccines, clean cars, and to avoid the asteroid named 2024 YR4, which, as of this writing, has a 3% chance of striking the Earth and causing immense death and destruction.

But we also need whimsy, silliness, and joy. We need the truth that the death of a loved one stings forever and that the sky is an oracle for our souls. Being creative is not about making money. If that is your primary goal, someone is always hiring economists. Creativity is about being our most human selves. It's about creating meaning and sharing our discoveries with others.

Creativity is telling stories by firelight when the sounds of the wolves in the wilderness drive sleep from our minds.

I SAW TRUTH
CRAWL OUT

A CROOKED
OAK TREE
HOLLOW

IN SEARCH
OF DINNER

. . .

It is noticing the patterns of nature and finding comfort in small joys and beauties in a society that is often dark and unjust. Two obstacles that stop most people from being more creative. One is imposter syndrome, and the other is not knowing where to start.

Imposter syndrome is nothing more than your fear of being seen, of not being seen, of failing, or of succeeding. It's a normal human reaction to stare into the void and try to explain what you've seen to strangers.

Not knowing where to start with creativity is the result of the normal human desire to know the end from the beginning—but that's not how stories work. The solution to both issues is to lean into your humanity. You cannot think your way out of a creative problem. You can only create your way out.

If you want to be more creative, look for signs. Hear voices in the middle of the night, get messages from the hoots of owls, and listen to ideas in the tick-tock of the clock or the babbling of the bath water. See your destiny in the stars, find faces in the clouds, and take dictation from the muses hidden in the steam coming off your morning latte.

The true beauty of creativity is that you are your own boss. Nobody has to give you permission to make something. You don't need a commission or credentials to create. It doesn't have to be your job, and what you make doesn't even need to be any good. The only requirement for being creative is to be human—your most human self.

Are you up to the task? If you've been waiting for a sign that now is the time to make something, consider this your sign. Go and make something right now!

CLOUDS PART
AND GATHER

SKY
CHANGES
LIKE A
MOOD RING

WORN BY
TEENAGE BOY

Chapter 15

Is This How You Stop Time?

The greatest lie in modern society is that we should all strive to optimize our lives, to become efficient in our personal and professional spheres. Miserable billionaires and life-hack gurus tell us the only way to combat the universal truth that our time is limited is to make the most of each second by discarding wasted movement and idle dreams. Their obsession with efficiency and optimization spills into their politics and personal lives, which is probably why so many of the wealthiest people in the history of the world are so angry all the time.

Efficiency is a lie for every human being. With our vestigial organs and internal redundancies, we are inefficient creatures from birth. Optimization is another fraud. Optimize our lives for what? You already know—for productivity, another unreal concept. A human life cannot be measured using cold calculations of the units produced over time.

A human life, any human life, is invaluable. A good life, one worth living, is not spent hoarding treasure like some cursed dragon or toiling away in a mine to help some dragon gain more loot. A good life should be measured in smiles, laughs, and sunsets.

But what about the problem of time? We all have an uncertain amount of time; our lifespans are limited. This is an argument for not wasting that life optimizing for productivity. This is an argument for skipping out on working for other people whenever you get the chance to pursue the true work of humanity: experiencing the world and other humans.

Instead of trying to count the seconds of my life as if time were gold coins and I was a miserly Ebenezer Scrooge, I work to stop time from flowing altogether. The secret to stopping time is to stop counting it. Do not look to the past with regret or the future with anxiety. Look to the moment you are right now, and it will stretch on for eternity.

I was not born with the ability to stop time. I spent much of my youth waiting for milestones to pass, looking for chances to escape my family, and stressing out about everything.

However, there were moments when I stumbled across the secret of time. In the twilight hours of a Northern California summer, we would scale the walls that blocked access to the culvert and the train tracks and wait for our ride. Freight trains would slow down as they came through our suburban town, and we would grab onto the ladders that hung from some of the cars, letting the train carry us for miles and miles, jumping off before it picked up too much speed, then finding ourselves someplace where new adventures awaited.

These illicit train rides would often take no time at all. We would make our way back home, and it was like coming out of the wardrobe, returning to the real world from Narnia. We had experienced endless adventures, but for the rest of the world, it was as if almost no time had passed at all.

THE RIVER OF TIME
ONLY STOPS FLOWING FOR THOSE
WITH NO PLACE TO GO

We were so consumed with living in the moment that we had stopped time. I am too old to jump trains. But I still have a love for getting trapped inside of moments, for stopping time. These days, I practice stopping time by walking along the Willamette (pronounced like it rhymes with "damn it") River and watching the seasons change. This is not efficient. I spend more time walking than I do writing or illustrating. My life is not optimized for work.

Instead, most days, I venture out to the river and let life flow around me. I have seen some of the world's great rivers. I have cruised on the Yangtze and Yellow Rivers of China. I have seen the mighty Mississippi from the sky. I have rafted, fished, and water-skied on many of the minor rivers of the Western United States. But no river has ever captured my heart like my local Willamette River has.

I've been walking its shores for twenty years and cannot remember what year I saw which wonder unless I recorded it with a poem, in which case I know the exact date. Each time I walk along the Willamette, I lose myself. Time stops being a concern.

Instead, I observe the river and life flow around me, letting myself become part of that flow.

Spring is my favorite time to walk along the Willamette because all of the rain keeps most of the people away. It's not that I don't like people, it's just that I'm selfish and enjoy having the river to myself. When I don my all-weather jacket and mud boots, I feel invincible. If you don't care about getting wet and dirty, there is nothing better than a hike in a torrential downpour.

Many days, I've returned to my car dripping wet and had to peel my jacket off and throw it in the backseat while rushing to get into the front seat, where my notebook waits for me to furiously write down ideas from my rain walk. Some of my best poems have been written in the car, with the heater blowing my notebook pages, my jacket dripping on the backseat floor, and rain pounding on the windshield.

Summer here is gloriously languid. With the kids out of school and the rain banished for a brief season, I have more chances to explore the river. Some places just aren't accessible when it rains every day. In summer I encounter fellow walkers and hikers, and more importantly, their dogs. There is just as much character and color to the canines along the river as is to their human companions.

More than once, I have rescheduled a client meeting so that I could stay longer watching the river. And every time, I have been richly rewarded for my laziness with beautiful sights and fleeting moments of kismet-fueled epiphanies. It's a good thing I work for myself because any sensible boss would've fired me long ago. I'm not built for employment. The fall is when the Willamette River Valley shows off. The explosion of glorious colors happens almost imperceptibly and then all at once.

The best hiking weather here is from mid-September through mid-October. The temperatures are mild, there is little rain, and most years, the wildfires have been extinguished.

BACHELOR EAGLE

SQUAWKS ABOUT HIS SOLITUDE

WHILE LOOKING FOR FISH

The migrating Canada geese are a common fall sight, as are several species of ducks, herons, and other waterfowl. Often, watching other people watching the birds is more interesting than the birds themselves. I hear snippets of intriguing stories full of betrayals avenged and tragedies overcome. The people you meet along the river in the fall are always in a good mood and eager to chat.

The rains return in winter. After the first big storm, many of my favorite trails become impassable for the season.

The River changes, too. It often breaks its banks and fills all of its sloughs. Its color transforms from blue to gray, reflecting the change in the sky and the amount of soil it carries downstream to the Columbia.

However, in winter, the mallard ducks are more active, and the bald eagles begin their nesting season. Every winter season is the same. Every winter season is different. Walking the river day after day, season after season, year after year, is not efficient.

If I wanted to optimize my exercise, I would get a treadmill. But on a treadmill, you cannot hear the bald eagles trilling to each other during nesting season. You cannot see a trout jump up and grab a morsel of grub from the river's surface. You cannot feel the rain pour down on your face. And you cannot see the subtle changes in color as fall descends again on the valley.

Walking the river has allowed me to live a thousand lives. Why would I want to be more efficient and squeeze in more work?

The reason our society worries so much about time, the reason billionaires hoard wealth, and the reason bosses everywhere try to manipulate people into being more productive is a raging fear of death.

Walking the river has taught me that you only need to fear death if you have failed to live life.

You can worry about efficiency and optimization all you like. I will be walking the river, learning to stop time instead.

Chapter 16

Stop Optimizing and Gamifying Your Life

The danger that humanity faces isn't that algorithms and robots will rise up and seize power. The threat we face is that we will voluntarily become indistinguishable from the algorithms and robots. Everywhere, from digital nomad gurus to the false prophets of productivity, we are taught how to optimize every aspect of our existence. You can find carefully scripted routines for your mornings, your sex life, and your bowel movements.

There is no aspect of human life that you couldn't be doing better. Our phones are littered with apps that help us "do better" by turning life into a series of mini-games and pinging us with alerts every hour of the day. Get a badge for reading seven days in a row! Complete a ring by taking lots of steps!

To paraphrase Jeff Goldblum's character, Ian Malcolm, in *Jurassic Park,* we're so busy studying how to optimize our lives that we never stop to consider if we should optimize our lives.

Optimization means making something the best it can possibly be. Shouldn't that be what we are all striving for, to live the best life we possibly can? One problem is that "best" is subjective, and optimization relies on objective processes. Most productivity hacks try to help you accomplish more in less time. But is that good? Does making more stuff for your boss make your life better? Does it even help your boss? Optimization and productivity are fossils. Management consultants created these concepts during the Industrial Revolution. Work doesn't work like that anymore.

If you are a knowledge worker, what does optimizing your productivity even mean? Do you need a waterproof notepad to write down all your shower thoughts?

Are you being productive when you have an idea for a piece of content for your business or employer while watching Netflix? Optimization is just another way for you to make more of your life about work instead of the work of being human. Most of the best things in life cannot be optimized.

Each one of us has a unique set of skills, life experiences, and environmental influences. No master routine will work for everyone. Getting up at 4 am might be great for a young, single Silicon Valley entrepreneur. But getting up at 4 am is beyond suboptimal when the second you get up, you will wake up a house full of children.

We do not all have the same twenty-four hours in a day. We do not all have the same obsession with getting rich. I would rather not take fancy vacations to expensive resorts if it means working sixty hours a week.

I'm happier walking in the woods for an hour each day and quitting work at three or four in the afternoon.

It's easy to spend so much time trying to improve everything in your life that you fail to take stock of what you love about it. If you constantly push yourself to get more work done, consume more information, eat the best diet, and exercise the best way, you are acting like a machine.

Human intelligence isn't designed for a life of optimization. That is why we try to trick ourselves into doing more by gamifying everything. We use the same psychological manipulation to push ourselves to do more work that slot machine manufacturers use to lure us into spending more money on a game we cannot win.

One of the worst elements of gamification culture is how we use it to track things we should enjoy. Do you need to track how many good books you read? Must you know precisely how many sunsets you watched? Does knowing exactly how many minutes you spent listening to that one artist make you enjoy their music more? Life isn't about being the best at everything. Life isn't about maximizing anything.

Life is about being human. It's about making mistakes, laughing, and loving. We all hope to become better, but constantly searching for the best increases anxiety and destroys happiness. There is an opportunity cost to everything in life. Our culture is biased towards evaluating only the easily calculable costs. You cost yourself money if you read a novel instead of sending three extra proposals to prospects. You can work out a formula to calculate exactly how much money you're losing. But what is the cost of making a few extra dollars instead of feeding your creativity and relaxing with a book? We don't know how to calculate that, so we "optimize" by being more productive and making more money.

Optimization also has no sense of enough. We get so caught up in trying to obtain more success, earn more money, and get more stuff done that we never stop to ask how much is enough.

Many of the practices you find on business blogs and magazines are about ways to save time so that you can make more money. They want you to waste less time. This assumes your time is fungible, that every second is equal to every other second. Some seconds are more precious than others. The actual waste would be to send another email instead of cuddling the one you love when they're experiencing a moment of pain.

One of my least favorite optimization hacks is listening to podcasts or audiobooks at higher speeds. When you listen to a podcast at a higher speed, you deny yourself the chance to ponder and process the information. We do not have a shortage of information; we have a shortage of analysis. You aren't gaining anything from this practice. What's your rush? Before you seek to optimize any area of your life, ask yourself what are you trying to make more time for? What are you sacrificing to become faster, stronger, and better? Instead of optimizing your life, try living it.

I went to the woods because I wished to live deliberately, to front only the essential facts of life, and see if I could not learn what it had to teach, and not, when I came to die, discover that I had not lived. I did not wish to live what was not life, living is so dear; nor did I wish to practice resignation, unless it was quite necessary. I wanted to live deep and suck out all the marrow of life, to live so sturdily and Spartan-like as to put to rout all that was not life, to cut a broad swath and shave close, to drive life into a corner, and reduce it to its lowest terms...

— Henry David Thoreau from *Walden*

I'm not saying we shouldn't try to be better. Self-improvement is one of the great drivers of humanity. But we need to stop obsessing about being the best. Optimization is a fool's game because it relies on a negative comparison. You will never measure up to other people's performance or to the idealized potential you see for yourself. Gradual self-improvement relies on a positive comparison. Are you better, even marginally, today than you were yesterday?

In the journey of life, the direction you're traveling in influences the quality of the life you lead more than the speed of your travel. Instead of trying to optimize your life, live your life. Breathe deeply, laugh, and love. Work hard and play hard. Ask interesting questions. Observe the world around you and live in the moment.

Automation is going to change the way we live. But many of us are reacting to automation by trying to out-optimize the algorithms. We react out of fear, and our reaction is making us more machine-like. The race to optimization is a race we cannot win. We still need human intelligence. AI does not create. It imitates. It might write haiku faster than me, but its lines are just remixes of the words of humans placed in an arrangement people are statistically likely to enjoy. The "poetry" of a large language model doesn't tell you what it feels or describe what moves your soul. There is no truth in a line of AI-generated art.

Think about the old folktales of John Henry or Paul Bunyan. These men went head-to-head with automation. They optimized their work, and they lost. John Henry died trying to lay more track than the machine, and the giant Paul Bunyan became an exile after failing to cut down more trees than a puny man with an automatic saw.

AI-powered automation could be a gift. It could allow us time to explore what makes us uniquely human. Things like art, curiosity, and relationships. Instead of automating the most tedious work tasks, we are using AI to speed up the demise of our planet to create schlock. A world where humans compete with AI by optimizing their productivity is a dystopia where humans and robots are indistinguishable. Stop optimizing and start living your life. It's the only way to keep from becoming a robot.

Chapter 17

Quitting is for Finishers

I love quitting. I frequently encourage my kids to quit, and I quit stuff all the time.

I come from a long line of people who believed in enduring to the end. They were diehards (literally). Some of my ancestors froze to death while crossing the American plains on the way to what they believed to be the promised land in the 1850s. Despite the signs of an early, ugly winter, they kept walking and pushing their handcart until some of them died. To them, enduring to the end was a religious requirement.

My father hated it when his children gave any signs of quitting. He felt quitting was a heinous character flaw. Walking away from something demonstrated a lack of integrity and a penchant for laziness. He firmly believed in the cliche that winners never quit and quitters never win.

Dad loved to tell us that the only people who ever accomplished anything were the ones who persevered. He had a point. Before you can be successful in any art, craft, skill, business, or physical feat, you have to work hard over a long period of time, and enjoy at least a little luck. However, the most successful people have also quit a lot of things.

Bill Gates dropped out of college, as did many other billionaire tech giants. Many of the most talented professional athletes quit college early. Many of your favorite artists and writers quit other careers before finding their true calling. Mark Twain deserted from the Confederate army, quit journalism, and half a dozen other jobs before becoming one of America's favorite novelists.

One of the most famous winners in the history of professional sports is Michel Jordan. He was also a quitter. Jordan led the Chicago Bulls to three NBA titles between 1991 and 1993. After years of getting creamed in the playoffs, Jordan was ascendant. He was winning every award possible. Nobody seemed poised to stop him or his Chicago Bulls from winning even more.

Jordan also had a lot of grief and personal issues to work through, so he quit basketball in 1995 to chase his dream of playing professional baseball. He was signed to a minor-league professional contract and was a serviceable player. Just making it to the minor leagues was a massive accomplishment. A tiny percentage of baseball players ever make it to that level. After a little more than a year, it was clear that Jordan was not a dominant baseball player and was unlikely to ever make the major leagues, so he quit baseball and returned to basketball.

Jordan would win three more NBA titles, cementing his status as one of the greatest athletes in any sport of all time. Would Michael Jordan have won those three additional NBA titles if he had stayed in the league? He was feeling burned out and bored. Quitting basketball and then quitting baseball to come back to basketball gave him the rest he needed to reach his full potential.

The only thing worse than quitting something too soon is sticking with something too long. Very few of our decisions around quitting are permanent. You can return to college if the band or startup fails. You can un-quit just about anything. Sometimes, you need a break and a change of perspective. You are also allowed to change your mind. The dreams you had as a teenager may not serve you in your thirties, forties, or beyond.

Starting in high school, I knew I wanted to be a lawyer. The plan was to go to law school and then get into politics. I rushed through college, only taking the classes that moved me closer to graduation, never taking anything just because I was curious. In undergrad, I interned in the U.S. Senate for Oregon's senator Gordon Smith. I realized I had no desire to work in politics, but I stuck to the plan anyway and went to law school.

I hated law school, but because it was so expensive, I thought I was better off just pushing through instead of wasting the tuition after just one year. The only thing I hated more than law school was practicing law. After almost nine years, I quit practicing law, causing a lot of havoc in my life. But, by quitting that dream from my teenage years, and muddling around for many years, I found happiness as a writer and illustrator, things that were not on my radar as a teenager or even in my twenties and early thirties.

How do you know when to quit? Your gut knows. How do you feel when you think about quitting? Does it bring feelings of relief or regret? If you feel relief, take that as your sign to move on. Looking back, I understand there were so many signs that the law was not the right path for me. The *Dramatic Literature* class I took as a freshman in college was fun and easy for me. My professor constantly praised my writing, but I was too focused on the plan.

When I think about quitting, I imagine nothing changing about my path. If I never get any better or have any more success with what I'm doing, would I still pursue it? Sometimes, the answer is yes. I am not raking in millions from my haiku practice. But it gives me joy, and so I continue to pursue it. I will write haiku and make haiku comics even if I'm the only person who reads them. Other times, I realize I don't want to arrive at the destination I'm working so hard to reach. The sunk costs are not worth it. I would be better off quitting and trying something else.

I've quit all kinds of things. Sometimes, during a freelance copywriting project, clients get a little squirrelly. If a client mistreats me, I quit the project midstream without guilt. The second I refund any unearned money, I feel a huge weight lifted from my soul. Life is too short, and there are too many other options for me to put up with that.

Some of the things that have caused me the greatest pain and suffering were things I didn't quit soon enough. I kept lawyering until I had a nervous breakdown, even though I was unhappy with the career choice from my first semester in law school. Sticking that out just cost me my health and a lot of money.

There are also things that I haven't quit. I published my first book in 2016, and almost nobody read it for five years. There were years when I had fewer than twenty people who cared anything about what I was creating. Now, more people are reading and supporting my essays, poetry, and comics than have ever read anything else I've ever done. Why do I keep hammering away at this when I've quit so many other things? The difference was when I thought about not making haiku comics anymore, I felt sorrow and pain. I'm compelled to work on this stuff. It's what drives me. I would, and have for years, do it for free and for an audience as small as a handful of friends and my four children.

Because I have persevered, grown my skills, and attracted more readers, doing the work is sweeter now than ever. I feel energized every time I sit down to write or draw. Hearing from readers about how my work makes them feel fuels me to get better and make more stuff. Over time, I have found not only greater happiness, but more opportunities. I have collaborated with so many different artists and writers. I have been on podcasts, and hundreds of thousands of people have read my work. While I once made things that five people might read, most of my work now is read by thousands of people each day. This growth, this success, is because I have stuck with my wild idea to combine poetry, comics, and essays.

What started as writing haiku almost every day turned into making haiku comics and other kinds of poetry comics. Then my background as a copywriter led me to start using my poetry comics as illustrations for my essays.

While my current career is the result of perseverance, I would never have been able to keep going with my strange art project if I hadn't quit many other things along the way. Lawyers have precious little time for poetry and comics. Along the way, I've also quit three newsletters, freelance copywriting twice, and I gave up writing non-fiction books and articles about freelancing.

If there is a secret to life, I think it might be to keep quitting things until you find something you can't quit.

Chapter 18

Living an Audaciously Mundane Life

We have created a culture that works to tear us apart from the inside. You've seen the stories and stats about how we are lonelier than ever, our teenagers are more neurotic than ever, and we hate each other more than ever. At the same time, thousands of books, podcasts, articles, and social media posts tell us how to be extraordinarily happy.

Scrolling on social media is an exercise in outrage. If social media apps were your only source of information, you would think that the only things we have an abundance of in this world are anger and inadequacy.

We scheme to make more money by being more productive with our side hustles. If you are not rich and taking fabulous vacations to fantastic destinations, you are losing.

Our culture tells us the only way to be happy is to be extraordinary. But unless you live in Lake Wobegon, where all the children are above average, it's impossible for most of us to live extraordinary lives.

We live in a time of deep dissatisfaction. In the United States, much of that dissatisfaction is driven by an intractable set of real problems. However, our huckster culture that peddles detox cures, minimalism, and get-rich-quick schemes also plays a significant part in generating a sense of isolation.

On top of this, we now have tech-bros trying to push AI as the next great solution to our economic woes. Of course, AI is just a high-tech game of three-card monte. Us regular people will never win playing that game.

If all of this sounds bleak, you must understand there is hope. But the way out of this situation requires a change in your mindset.

When the game is rigged, the only way to win is not to play.

If you want to live a life of contentment and happiness, you need to be brave enough to fully enjoy a mundane existence.

You have to live an audaciously mundane life.

I'm a late Gen-Xer. That means my parents were Baby Boomers, and my grandparents were all survivors of the Great Depression and World War II. On my dad's side, my grandparents were both teachers who also owned a gas station and grocery store in rural Idaho attached to their house. On my mom's side, her stepfather was a master plasterer, and her mom was an administrative assistant at the state hospital.

My grandparents left little in the way of an inheritance when they passed. They were never rich, but they were some of the happiest people I've ever met because they knew how to be happy with enough. They knew how to find the small joys in life.

They were extraordinarily ordinary.

None of them ever ran a marathon or took a trip around the world. My dad's mom kept a beautiful flower garden, and my mom's mother raised a variety of vegetables in her backyard.

My grandpas would take me for long drives around the Idaho countryside on hot summer afternoons, telling me stories about their lives and showing me where our people used to live.

When my grandparents weren't entertaining grandchildren or on road trips staying with relatives, they played cards or dominoes with their neighbors and friends from church.

There were no cruises or sports cars.

For most of human existence, that was how we all lived. We worked, played, and then we died. Life used to be simple.

The truth is, it still can be. If you are willing to lower your expectations and open your eyes, you can lead a wonderful life just being ordinary. Instead of longing for a life you've seen on Instagram, you can go outside and watch the sunset where you live for free every night.

Instead of working three side hustles, you can learn to shrink your lifestyle. Your work doesn't have to change the world or be your life's purpose. You can just work hard enough to pay the bills and put food on the table.

You can make paintings of what you can see outside your window, and never try to sell them on Etsy. Instead, you could paint for your own enjoyment, no matter how bad you are at it initially. When you have too many of your paintings around the house, you could give them away to friends and family.

There are so many things to see right where you live that you've yet to discover. There are flowers, birds, and buildings that are waiting for you to notice them. They may not make for a viral Instagram post, but if you open all of your senses, you will discover hidden wonder among the mundane things of your neighborhood.

My first experience with living an audaciously mundane life was the pandemic. We had four kids at home, and suddenly we had lots of time together. We learned to be more creative. We invented games, played outside more, and found peace doing chores.

Instead of seeing life as an endless cycle of drudgery, we saw each day as a fresh chance to make life interesting.

Since that time, I've worked to maintain a sense of simplicity. I take walks in my community every day, looking for signs of wonder. I always find them.

I don't look to social media for inspiration. I am not striving to live the life of an influencer. Instead, I'm seeking the sacred in the mundane. When cooking for my family or doing the dishes, I focus on what I am doing instead of what I could be doing. I'm slowly shedding the envy and FOMO that make happiness impossible.

I also create something every day. It might be a poem or a collage. Most of the things I make are not for work or a side hustle. I create for the sheer joy of creating.

When I bring my attention to what is happening around me, I find joy in the mundane. My curiosity leads me to learn more about why the woodpeckers love to peck our chimney each spring. I notice patterns in the weather and weeds that I've missed, even though I've lived in the same place for more than twenty years.

From the outside, my life looks dull. I spend most of my day working on maintaining our home, raising children, and writing to pay the bills.

In our home, there is always laughter. We have enough food to eat and live in one of the most beautiful places on the planet. Every day, I cook and clean, and every day I see something wonderful.

I may not ever be able to retire or visit all of the places in the world I long to see, but every day I draw breath, I can find contentment in my life and wonder in a world that is always changing, even as it rotates through the same four seasons each year.

It takes a certain kind of audacious courage to love living a mundane life. But if you're brave enough to give up a life of endless striving and chasing hits of outrage, you can find peace and happiness in the ordinary.

Chapter 19

You Are a Generative Human Intelligence

We exist in a strange moment in history when capitalism is weaponizing technology to get us to give up our humanity. Many of the most powerful and popular new technological gadgets and apps aren't designed to make you better at something. They are designed to do something for you, to convince you to give up a part of your humanity.

There is a push to convince you that you are not creative enough, that you don't have time to write your story or paint that idea you got from that strange dream. These are lies.

Creativity is at the core of what it means to be human. You are creative. You don't have to be an artist or a writer to be creative. You just have to be human. When you decide to remix two nights of leftovers into street tacos so that your family will think they are eating something new and not leftovers, you are being creative. The moment you invent a game for your kids to play, you are being creative. When you lie to get out of work or to avoid a boring meeting, you are being creative.

You do have enough time to be creative. The real problem is you don't want to be bad at being creative. You want an app that will do it for you so that you don't have to be a beginner, so that you don't have to feel uncomfortable about making ugly things. But our apps don't help us do things. They do things for us. They do things to us. The navigation apps on our phones don't improve our navigation skills. Instead, we completely outsource that task to the phone and never learn our way around our neighborhood. AI writing assistants don't teach you to be a better writer. They just write for you. They stop you from thinking about how to best communicate with another human being and instead train you to trust the machine. The current stage of technology is delivering learned helplessness.

We move forward as individuals, societies, and as a species, through creativity. Creative people—the weirdos—see the world as it could be and then reverse engineer the way forward in their imaginations.

The master plan for generative AI is for technology companies to sell us progress on a subscription. There are lots of ways true AI could be useful to us, but mostly, we are using inferior generative AI technologies to slowly phase out our creativity. The robot uprising isn't a revolution. It's a slow-moving corporate takeover, and we are fully cooperating.

The funny thing about humans is that we love to create, and we are also terribly resistant to change and discomfort. One of the most powerful uses of our creativity is to make people uncomfortable. That includes your parents, your teachers, your bosses, your political leaders, and yourself. Progress is a form of change, and change is always uncomfortable.

New problems are not solved by applying old solutions. Progress is not made by doing what has always worked in the past. But what happens when we no longer know how to do things? When we lose the ability to write for ourselves, to create for ourselves, how do we solve problems? We pay someone else to solve them for us.

GROW OLD
TOGETHER

NONSEQUENTIAL
LOVE STORY

MEET CUTE
ON MOON

You can already see our culture heading down this path. We are all essentially cyborgs. We use our phones as a synthetic memory to store directions and details about our loved ones. It's not that technology is bad. The issue is how many of us use technology thoughtlessly. How easily we give up our autonomy and humanity to technology companies that exist to make profits, not to make our lives better.

Human creativity is about disrupting the status quo, and that makes people uncomfortable, especially the people in charge, the ones who benefit the most from the status quo. We are at a critical juncture. We can either outsource our ability to change ourselves and our communities to Silicon Valley, or we can take back our humanity and start creating the kinds of solutions we want to see.

But first, you must believe in your own creative powers. Any time you have made a change in your life, it has been driven by your creativity. You figured out how to break an old habit or make a new habit. You created a new path for yourself. If you want to change the world, you must nurture your creativity. Don't think that you are not creative. If you are alive, you are creative—even if you never do anything "creative", that power sits dormant inside of you. You can unleash it at any time.

Creativity looks different for everyone. Some dance, some sing, some write music, and some play music. Many write or draw. Others organize or carve wood or make shadow puppets. Humor is a form of creativity, as is teaching.

The tech oligarchs and the fascists do not want you to believe that you are creative because creative people make them uncomfortable. Creative people aren't satisfied with what is and are always wondering what could be. Creative people look behind the curtains and think for themselves. Creative people not only have hope, but they also inspire others to have hope, and that hope is fatal to tyrannical systems. If you want to see a better world, you can start by unleashing your creativity, not as a side hustle or productivity hack, but to enjoy your life more.

Do you remember how it felt to create as a child? Do you remember making messes and laughing? Do you remember singing at the top of your lungs or spinning around in the front room until you collapsed to the floor? You can feel that again. All you have to do is get uncomfortable. You must be willing to look silly. To be creative, you must embrace your inner weird. Once you accept that, nothing can stop you. The more creative activities you try, the more ideas you will have in other areas.

If you want to change the world, you must be creative, you must be weird. That's the only way. Normal people have never once changed the world. You don't need generative AI to bring your ideas to life. You are an extremely powerful generative human intelligence. You can learn to paint, draw, write, or make films. You can and should learn new creative skills for the joy of learning and creating—not as the means to getting rich.

It doesn't matter if your new vase is lumpy or if your painting of a horse looks more like your dog. The power and joy of creativity are in the doing of the thing. If you love the activity enough, you will find the time to do it more and get more skilled at it. There is magic to doing things you love solely for fun. It nourishes your soul, and it eats away at the power of the massive corporations and oligarchs that want to extract value from you to pad their bank accounts.

I promise you that if you embrace your creativity, you will change the world. Maybe not for everyone, but you will change it for someone, and that someone will be forever grateful to you. Now is the time to double down on your humanity by making stuff for the sheer joy of making things. What do you have to lose? Shake off the shackles of conformity and make some big, beautiful messes. You and your world will never be the same.

Chapter 20

Losing Yourself in the Patterns of Nature

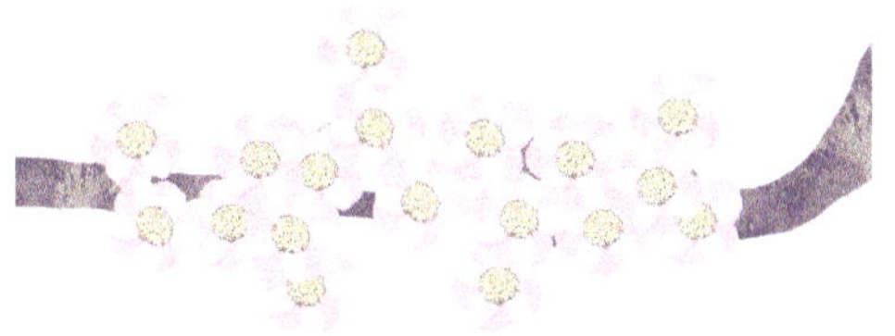

The world is not falling apart at the seams. I know, I know. Look at the news! Our civilization might be unwinding, but the world is not falling apart. Despite our determined efforts to despoil planet Earth, the planet herself isn't going anywhere anytime soon.

We talk about the end of the world, but Earth with her mountains, oceans, plant and animal life, and glorious sunrises and sunsets will outlast all of us. The climate crisis is more about the end of humanity than it is the Earth. It's the end of our dominion, not the end of the planet. Though to be fair, we are taking a number of other species down with us at the moment.

That doesn't mean that we shouldn't work to reverse course. We should work to limit climate change and find a way to live in harmony with the Earth and in peace with one another. I'm deeply committed to these aims.

Walking around feeling like we are doomed will not help change anything. Hope is an essential ingredient for change. If you don't hope for a better future, why bother agitating for change? One thing we humans excel at is centering our own experiences.

You and I both think we're the center of the universe. We aren't even cogs in the great gearbox of the infinite universe.

I find hope by losing myself in the patterns of nature. My outlook improves greatly once I stop obsessing over my feelings and start noticing the wonder in the world.

Some of the most magnificent events in nature are the easiest to overlook because they are so frequent. Every day, you get to witness a sunrise and a sunset. Despite these being daily occurrences, each one is different from any previous sunrise or sunset.

Poets often use sunrises as symbols of birth and renewal. To me, the sunrise is better understood as a transition. Life is an endless cycle of days and nights, successes and failures, and rest and responsibilities. The sunrise is the moment when we shift from one thing to another. When I watch the sunrise, it's hard not to feel a call to action. Now is the time to make the art, talk to the attractive stranger, or plant the sapling in the yard.

Sunsets are also a marker of change. It's the time when you take accountability for how you spent your day, bask in the glow of the twilight sky, and move on to your nocturnal activities. For me, sunset is a signal for preparation and recuperation. Inspiration's whispers are the most seductive as the sun slinks down and the stars begin to pierce the creeping darkness.

My most important creative and mindfulness practice is to write haiku as often as possible. So far, I've written more than 4,000 of these tiny poems. That means I've written hundreds accounts of sunrises and sunsets. None of the poems are the same, but I do find I come back to the same themes over and over again.

I lose myself in these patterns so that later I can step back and discover what I'm truly feeling. Not surprisingly, sunrises and sunsets show up frequently in my comics as well. How can I not try and capture the strange changes to the sky as our sun's celestial movements change the whole sky like a dimmer switch in my grandma's dining room?

One summer evening, our family was staying at the beach with our friends. One of their sons-in-law said one of the most heartbreaking things I've ever heard. A gaggle of us were gathered in the back of our beach house rental, watching the Pacific sunset that inspired the haiku comic above, when he announced he was going inside because he'd seen plenty of sunsets.

Maybe it was the arrogance of youth. Perhaps he was making an excuse so he could take care of some work responsibilities without guilt. But I had been alive for at least twice as many sunsets as him, and I could not, and still cannot, imagine willingly rushing away from a beach sunset to go inside.

Each sunset is the same in the way each human is the same. There's a common set of features, but the miracle is in the small differences. The sun comes up and goes back down regardless of how much attention we give it. The same is true of the human events of each day.

We each only have a limited capacity for attention. What if, at least twice a day, you took a sabbatical from breaking news, push notifications, and demands for your attention and just watched our local star's comings and goings? What if you allowed yourself to do nothing and just be in awe for a few minutes at the start and end of your day? What kind of changes would it make in your mood and ability to focus the rest of the day?

Losing yourself in the patterns of nature allows you to decenter your own limited human experience and puts you in touch with nature, with the infinite universe, for at least one moment.

Allowing yourself to watch the most regular and awesome spectacles of our planet, the sunrise and the sunset, every chance you get, opens your soul to hope and breaks the shackles of doom our civilization is intent on locking onto all of us.

The world is not ending, and if you are willing to lose yourself in nature, you will begin to see new ways to reform and rebuild the relationship we humans have with the planet and one another.

The seeds of hope can be planted anew with each sunrise and each sunset, if you're willing to just sit and stare once in a while.

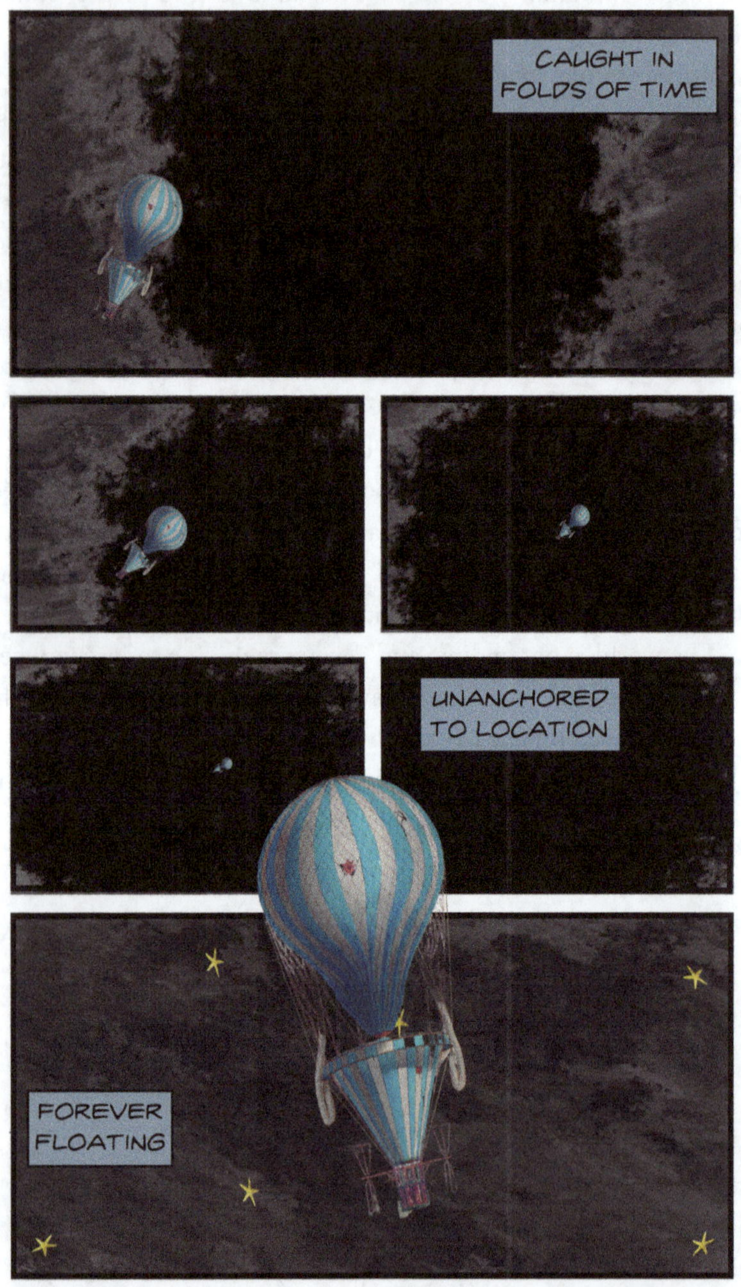
CAUGHT IN
FOLDS OF TIME
UNANCHORED
TO LOCATION
FOREVER
FLOATING

Chapter 21

Your Ideas Are Not Precious

The hard truth about any creative endeavor is that a good idea is essential, but not sufficient, to bring something to life. Many aspiring writers, painters, musicians, and film-makers never become artists because they are stuck waiting for the right idea or are obsessed with a single idea. They cannot move forward until the ideal idea is perfectly realized.

Having an idea for a thing is intoxicating. It's one of life's great pleasures, up there with waking up after sex with the right person and the last bite of a perfect meal. But having an idea is not the same as doing the thing. The difference between the amateur and the professional is that the amateur simultaneously takes ideas too seriously and doesn't take them seriously enough.

Ideas are everywhere. In the moment, it's almost impossible to tell if an idea is good or not. Ideas need time to percolate, to ferment in the stew of your experiences, memories, and knowledge. Ideas change as they collide with other ideas.

Amateurs latch too tightly onto one idea, scared to share it lest someone else "steal" it, and unable to move forward with their craft unless it relates to the one specific idea. But ideas are not precious. A precious gemstone is precious because it is rare. Ideas are not rare. Ideas are everywhere. Not even good ideas are precious. They are everywhere, too. You hurt your creativity when you hoard ideas and refuse to share them.

Taking ideas too seriously stunts creativity. You become obsessed with making the thing exactly like you imagined it. Becoming an artist is about narrowing the gap between what you imagine and what you make. However, there will always be a gap. When you refuse to finish a work because it is not perfect, you never get better. You never narrow the gap.

Ideas are living things, independent of us. They are in the air. This is one reason simultaneous discovery is so common. Often, several movies will come out around the same time. This is not because someone is stealing ideas. Rather, this happens because sometimes ideas are in the zeitgeist, and different versions of those ideas strike multiple people.

Artists know that if they don't act on an idea, someone else will. Elizabeth Gilbert talks about an experience like this in her book on creativity, *Big Magic*. She had an idea for a novel that she felt she couldn't undertake because of personal issues, and a year later, another author published their version of the same concept. Gilbert didn't think her idea had been stolen. Rather, she understood that the idea was right for the moment and found someone ready to execute it.

The difference between an aspiring artist and a working artist is that working artists respect ideas enough to start taking imperfect steps to bring them to life. They also respect ideas enough to let some of them go. Not every idea that occurs to you is right for you. The more you practice being sensitive to the world around you, the more ideas you will discover. I don't know a single professional artist who doesn't have far more ideas than they have the capacity to execute. When it comes to being a working artist in any field, having ideas is the easiest part.

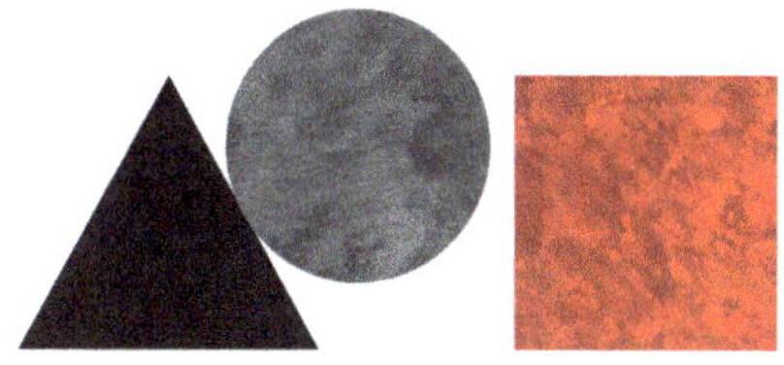

The real work of creativity is transmuting an idea into a thing. An idea for a script is not the same as a script. Like every author, I've met people who, once they discover I've published books, gleefully tell me they have a great idea for a book. They just haven't gotten around to writing it yet. As if the writing of the book is the trivial part, and the real work is the idea. Having an idea for a book does not make you an author.

This same phenomenon plays out with AI. So many people, including a fair number of studio executives, believe that they are artistic geniuses who are only kept from greatness because they lack the talent to make a movie. They want to use AI to shortcut all the actual work involved in making a movie. Having an idea for a movie doesn't make you a filmmaker.

If you use AI to do all the work involved in writing a book, making a movie, or creating a drawing, what do you have to be proud of? You haven't done anything. You had an idea and outsourced the work to AI. Art is in the execution of an idea, not in the having of an idea.

If you want to be an artist, learn the skills to be an artist. You do not need an MFA (Masters of Fine Arts) to be a writer. You don't need to go to art school to be an artist. You do need to learn how to do things. Writers write and painters paint. The more you do the thing, the better you will get at it.

The more technical skills you have, the easier it will be to bring your ideas to life in a way that is close to what you imagined. Narrowing the gap requires iteration and perspiration. You have to keep at it.

I've been a working writer for more than thirteen years. I'm better today than I was when I started. I have no formal training in creative writing. However, I read obsessively, and am deeply curious about what makes a piece of writing work. Like a developing auto mechanic, I disassemble and reassemble other people's sentences and paragraphs to see what makes them hum.

The ideas I work with are not any better than what I had when I started, but my ability to harness those ideas has improved. Several years ago, I had an idea for making poetry comics. I had no visual arts skills. I had stopped any kind of painting or drawing when I was humiliated by my art teacher in middle school.

Mr. Emery told me in front of the class that I was so bad at art it was probably best if I didn't even go to museums to look at art. Visual art wasn't for me. But I liked the idea of poetry comics. I couldn't afford to hire an illustrator, and I loathed involving someone else in a project I was sure would be a commercial failure.

That left me with one option. Learn to become a good enough illustrator to make my ideas a reality. My illustration work is not polished, but I have my own process, visual language, and style. I've been commissioned by people to do illustration work for them. Somehow, much to my surprise, I became not only a professional writer but also a professional illustrator.

It takes a lot of work to learn the skills required to execute my ideas. I still work on my writing and illustration skills. Just like musicians continue to practice their instruments, I continue to practice my craft. But the practice is not onerous; it's joy. It's play. It's life.

If you yearn to be an artist of any kind, spend more time practicing your craft than you do worrying about ideas. There will always be ideas. We live in a universe of infinite ideas. But there will always be only a finite number of people willing to do the work to bring some of those ideas into the physical world.

Those people are called artists.

Chapter 22

There is No Secret to Success

Whenever Steve Martin is asked about what it takes to succeed in the entertainment industry, he gives advice I used to detest. Martin always responds, "Be so good they can't ignore you."

I used to hate that line because I thought it focused too much on talent and ignored the reality that luck plays an outsized role in success. I hated it because it also ignores the fact that we all start at different points. Having a parent who is even a C-list celebrity gives you a leg up if you want to be in the entertainment industry. Over time, I've softened my criticism of his advice. I still believe luck and privilege play an outsized role in success, especially in the arts and entertainment industry. But I don't think Martin is talking about talent anymore. He's talking about work.

I think what Steve Martin meant was that you have to do the thing you want to be noticed for. You cannot control luck, who your parents are, or where you were born. The only things you can control are your effort and your attitude.

I still think luck plays an underappreciated role in any kind of success, but the more you play the game, the more likely you are to catch a lucky break. This is the real message of Malcom Gladwell's book *Outliers*. While many people focus on the so-called 10,000-hour rule, Gladwell's point was not so much about hitting a magic time threshold as it was that people who have outsized success also tend to have put in an extraordinary number of repetitions of their core skills.

If you spend most of the year touring as a stand-up comedian, you are much more likely to be in the right place at the right time than someone who only does stand-up in front of the bathroom mirror. You will also be much better at stand-up comedy because you will have done your reps.

Success in any endeavor not only requires some degree of luck, but it also requires some volume of effort. Not every person who has shot 10,000 baskets in practice will make it as a professional basketball player. But every NBA player has shot at least 10,000 baskets by the time they reach that level. Effort and tenacity are more strongly correlated with success than luck. The advice "fake it until you make it" is backwards. You must make it until you don't have to fake it.

You must do the thing you want to do so many times that you cannot imagine doing or being anything else. Writers write, painters paint, and musicians make music. If your dream is to be a novelist, the path forward is not to fake being a novelist. It's to do the things that novelists do, mainly write novels.

Instead of doing the work to reach our goals or make our dreams come true, most of us look for shortcuts or excuses. We let ourselves off the hook. If we never try our best, we don't have to feel bad about not becoming who we wanted to be. We can blame the system for our lack of success.

One of my earliest freelance writing gigs was creating sales copy for a success guru. The success business was a side project for him; his day job was in finance. He took a market-based approach to teaching about success. There were tons of people telling you how easy it was to be successful. He did the opposite.

If most self-help authors seek to uplift you, he wanted to punch you in the mouth. The client's business never earned more than a thousand dollars a month, and last I heard, he had shut the whole thing down.

I often wondered what kept his business from taking off. He had a catchy concept and brand. He knew who his target market was. His marketing was strong (even the stuff I didn't write, lol). But he never grew beyond a small group of followers.

A few years ago, I reached out to him as I was thinking about making some changes in my writing career. I asked him about the success business, and he told me his theory of why it failed.

He said he first blamed the market. People didn't like hard truths. Then he said he stopped lying to himself. The reason it never scaled was that he didn't practice what he preached. He was telling people they needed to work hard, but he was obsessed with growth hacking. His final verdict was that the business failed because he lost patience and failed to put in the work.

It's easy to look at anyone who seems successful to us and feel like everything fell into place so quickly for them. To the beginner, all success looks like a lightning strike. We start to think that if we can just figure out how to be in the right place at the right time, success will find us. This is a lie.

All success is long-tail success. Everyone who has become successful has put in a lot of work. Eventually, all the hard work builds up momentum, and they burst onto the scene.

What can you control? It's easy to fall in love with the myth of the lottery winner or the lightning strike. How great would it be if one day someone in a nice suit showed up at your door and declared that they're here to discover you? Some AI-powered program identified you as a person of great potential, even though so far you haven't done anything. Then they hand you a suitcase full of cash and tell you to go and create your vision. That sounds amazing—it's also never happened to anyone anywhere.

You can't control when lightning will strike. Some people do get lucky, but you can't replicate that. However, if you look closely, almost everyone who does get lucky has put in a lot of work. The other obstacle people face in becoming a writer, or any other kind of artist, is that the dream is often not just about doing the thing, it's also about making a certain amount of money.

You cannot control how others will receive your work. For a professional artist, the reaction of the audience is almost beside the point. The point is to do and share the thing.

The arts are not a get-rich-quick scheme; they aren't even a get-rich-slow scheme. The arts are a pathway to a more interesting life and becoming a more fulfilled human being. If you want a lot of money, there are many more efficient ways of going about it than becoming an artist. If you want to be an artist of some kind, it means doing whatever it takes so that you can make your next piece of art.

Being a professional artist means practicing your craft relentlessly. It means doing the doing the damn thing and sharing the damn thing over and over again. It might mean having a day job that pays the bills so you can create. It might mean doing work you don't like so you can make art you love. Being a professional artist in today's economy means learning how to string multiple income streams together so you can afford to make more art.

If that sounds like torture, perhaps you don't want to be a professional artist. That's great! You can still be a hobbyist. Having art as a hobby is good for your soul and will probably be better for your physical and mental health. Not everything is meant for everyone.

While anyone can become a professional artist in some capacity, the only people who should pursue the arts as a profession are those who have no choice. If you want to be wildly successful, getting up two hours before dawn, drinking three raw eggs each morning, or writing your to-do list in Latin aren't going to get you there. There are no success hacks. You have to do the work that you want to be noticed for.

The great news is that the internet has made it easier than ever for you to create. Are you into comedy? Art? Writing? You have so many different platforms and channels where you can share your work. You don't even have to work for free. This is the golden age of monetizing talent.

You are in control of your work ethic. You are in control of when you decide to quit. Stop looking for a secret map to the city of gold. It doesn't exist. Just do the thing. Then keep doing the damn thing.

Have you ever seen a child learn to walk? It's a disaster. Children don't just wake up one day and decide to walk. They start learning to walk the day they're born. Babies are observing everything and taking in information. After a few months, they want to locomote. They don't have the coordination or muscle tone to walk, so they crawl. Some babies don't even do that. They scooch. They spend countless hours crawling and scooching across the floor, watching adults and older kids walk. Eventually, they start pulling themselves up on furniture. At first, gravity grabs them back down to the ground more often than they succeed in getting up. After mastering pulling themselves up, they start trying to toddle between different pieces of furniture. After nine, ten, or thirteen months, they can walk independently. They still fall dozens of times a day.

Babies don't quit trying to walk. They don't know that's an option. Every child walks at their own pace. Some are faster, and some are slower, but every healthy child eventually gets there. Looking at a group of adults, you could never guess which ones took longer to walk and which ones were early walkers. It all balances over time. Success in any field is like that. You have to wobble, fall, and keep getting back up. Success and I are strangers, but failure and I are old friends.

When I have had success, it's because I've shown up every day to do the work. Until my desire to succeed is stronger than my desire to be comfortable, I won't have the strength or patience to put in the work. If you look back at the successes you've had in life, you will also find that you put in a lot of work before you ever made any headway.

We all want to be wildly successful as quickly as possible. If you're really in a hurry, the best thing you can do is work harder. If you're trying to make it as a cartoonist, draw twice as much every day as you think you need to. Send out pitches every week. Draw and share your work constantly. The truth that we don't want to face is that almost everyone who is successful has put in the work. Some people have unfair advantages. You can't control that. You can control how hard you work.

It's tempting to create goals to measure our success. Most of the time, we set goals that are out of our control. You can't control whether an agent will sign you or not. You can control how much work you produce and how many pitches you send out. When you focus on the process of your work instead of the goals, you get more done. You are also less likely to quit in frustration. The work itself becomes the goal. When you put process over goals, you learn faster, you enjoy the work more, and in the end, you do better work.

There is enough room in the world for you to be successful. The question is, do you have enough patience and are you willing to work hard enough to be successful? There's only one way to know for sure. You have to buckle down and get started.

You have to do the thing.

I IMBIBED
MOONBEAMS

AND FEASTED
UPON SUNSETS

TO HEAL FROM
LIFE'S STINGS

Chapter 23

Finding Pockets of Joy in an Angry World

As a child, the most often repeated feedback I received was that I was too sensitive. Nobody ever had any actionable advice on how I might become less sensitive. All those scolding adults wanted was for me to be quiet and learn to suppress the feelings that were always bubbling just under the surface. I never did learn how to be less sensitive. As I close in on the half-century mark on this beautiful blue marble, I've finally begun to believe that being sensitive is more blessing than curse.

However, that doesn't change the fact that this world is not made for sensitive types. We live in an angry world, full of bullies, energy vampires, and other dangers. Prophets of doom call down apocalypses, both real and imagined, all over social media. Every corner of the internet makes a mockery of hope and works hard to monetize your outrage.

Is it any wonder that anxiety is at an all-time high in our society? To survive, you either adapt to accept the tyranny of fear, suppressing your feelings and dulling your senses, or you must develop some way to at least momentarily escape the loud, angry madness. I choose not to accept a world ruled by the fear and anger of others. As Henry Miller wrote in *The Colossus of Maroussi,* "There is no salvation in becoming adapted to a world which is crazy."

The only option is to learn how to build your own emotional shelter from the storm. Fortunately, you are already equipped to do that. You can find pockets of joy in each day to give you a reprieve from the fear and anger echoing from all of our screens. We may live in an angry world, but we also live in a beautiful world of quiet, spectacular wonders. Humans and the rest of nature are capable of sublime displays of pure joy that you can bathe in, if you're paying attention.

You must learn to notice what you notice. Our brains are pattern-recognition machines. The same mechanism that causes you to notice a newly-learned word everywhere, or to see the same model of car you just looked at last week on the road each day, can be used to find more joy. You must train your brain to see wonder. Once you choose to look for wonder, you will see it everywhere. Even the most mundane day holds tiny pockets of joy.

You have the power to choose what you give your attention to. I'm not advocating for you to completely remove yourself from the world and live as a hermit on a mountain. It's critical for the health of democracy and our communities that you stay aware of what is happening. However, you do not need news alerts every half hour.

Constantly fretting about the minute-by-minute outrages does not make you a better citizen. Instead, it cripples your ability for mindful engagement and thoughtful action.

Remember, the fear and outrage are the most easily monetizable emotions. Many influencers and media companies want to keep you dysregulated, not as a way to prompt you to meaningful action, but as a way to keep you paralyzed and profitable for them. Give yourself, and those close to you, the gift of mindfulness. Take a break from the torrent of information and quietly notice what is happening around you.

Watch the sunset, look at the squirrels in the park, and smile at the children laughing in line at the ice cream truck. Take your focus off your emotions and thoughts, and soak in some of the wonders happening around you. Your life is too short to spend all of it angry and anxious.

I've found that just looking for wonder is not enough. I've developed a creative and spiritual practice to write a haiku about the wonders I see. It's my way of cataloging the pockets of joy I find so that I can turn to them when the world feels especially harsh. Spending a few moments in these pockets of joy gives me the strength to live in this world without having to dull my senses. It allows me to continue caring, without drowning in the world's sorrows.

We cannot afford for you to give up or give in to the forces that want you either outraged or apathetic. If you want to change the world, you must have some way to see all that is good, not just all that is awful. Lasting change is most often not made by those with the most intensity of feeling, but by those with the greatest persistence. Tyrants and oppressors of all kinds want you to get so angry that you burn out and drop out, so they can continue to amass power.

The simple act of noticing the moon during the daylight hours, or the whimsical way your neighbor's dog has to circle a spot of lawn three times before peeing, allows your soul to rest. Wonder fuels your compassion and silences your anxiety. Find pockets of joy in an angry world by paying attention to the small details of the world. Something as trivial as grass growing between the cracks of a city sidewalk offers you a chance to be grateful. That moment of attention to a small wonder will radically change the way you feel about the rest of your day.

What will you choose to do? Will you choose to adapt to a crazy world, or will you fight for a better future? I hope you will stay sensitive. I hope you will refuse to give in to outrage or apathy. If you want to stay in the fight, you must learn to find pockets of joy in each day. Your sensitive soul needs moments to shelter, rest, and recharge. Quiet joy in the face of tyranny is resistance. Noticing the wonders of the world allows you to persist in that resistance.

Chapter 24

How to Get Unstuck

Have you ever been stuck on the side of the road? There's nothing more frustrating than watching the world drive by while your car is motionless, broken in a way you might not even be able to fix on your own. When you're dealing with a car issue, you can call a tow truck or get some roadside assistance to get you back on your way. What happens when it's your life that feels broken? What do you do when you're stuck? There's no roadside assistance for a midlife crisis.

There are a lot of events that can lead to you feeling stuck. Getting fired, the death of someone close, realizing you hate your job, a failed romantic relationship, financial problems, becoming a parent, and just about any other type of life event can leave you feeling lost and alone. The feeling of being stuck in life is always rooted in fear. You are afraid of making the wrong decision. You don't know what to do because you think you have made bad decisions in the past that have led you to your current predicament, and you're afraid of spending more time going the wrong way. You are afraid of failing, or you're afraid of succeeding.

ROCKET'S VIOLENT
PUSH OFF THE ONLY WAY TO
ESCAPE GRAVITY

The problem is, even when you come to accept that your fear of failure or fear of success is what is holding you back, that fear is still there. You can't think it away. What you need is a little positive momentum. You don't need to solve all of your problems right now. You just need to start doing something differently. Instead of trying to figure out your entire life, focus on one of these nine strategies for getting unstuck. Not every strategy will work for you, but at least one of these will. If you keep doing things the way you've always done them, you will remain trapped in the same habits and stuck with the same sense of boredom and dissatisfaction.

In the end, the only way to get unstuck is to do something, anything, even the wrong thing. How do I know? I've been stuck on the side of the road both literally and metaphorically many times. The first time I questioned everything was when I had a nervous breakdown and quit the practice of law. I had no idea what I was going to do next. After recovering from cancer and other related illnesses, instead of feeling a sense of clarity and gratitude, I felt lost and like I was wasting my life.

There have been many other smaller moments as well, but each time I eventually got unstuck. But it was always gradual, and nobody else ever came to my rescue. If you're stuck, you can get unstuck. But first, you're going to have to try some new things.

Movement matters more than direction. Your brain loves to control you. There's safety in being stuck. That's one reason why all you can think about is how there is danger in every direction. That's why no choice feels right. Your brain doesn't want you to change. Change is scary. When you're stuck, the direction you head matters far less than the fact that you are moving at all. It's a bit like this exchange between Alice and the Cheshire Cat:

If you don't know where you want to go in life, then it doesn't matter what direction you go in. Just do something. It doesn't have to be the one right choice. Take the job you're unsure about, take the class that seems interesting, try a different career. The worst that can happen is that it doesn't work out. You already know what that feels like. At least you will have done something. Every time you try something, you make it easier to try something else. You learn new skills and meet new people that may help you in surprising ways later in life.

Don't try to make the right choice, just make any choice. Movement matters more than direction. Do it scared. Humans are a risk-averse species. That's why you're stuck. You're scared of taking a risk. If you weren't scared, you would do something. Do you know the difference between people with insane amounts of confidence and you?

The people with confidence, the people who are doing scary things, are also scared. They just do it scared. Life is an adventure. A journey without any danger or obstacles is an errand, not a quest. *You* are on a quest.

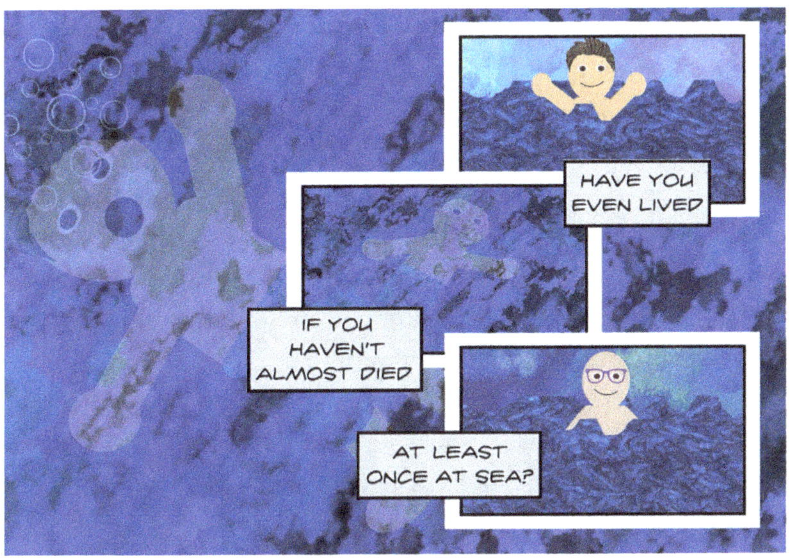

The funny thing about fear is that it's at its peak before you do the thing. Stage fright goes away once you say your first line. The water feels cold until you get used to it. If you want to get unstuck, decide you are going to start doing things scared. You'll be shocked by how far you can go, even when you're afraid.

You need to notice what you notice. Stop focusing on all the big things. Instead of trying to figure out relationships, career, and happiness, start looking at the small things in life. What patterns keep showing up? Do you feel excited when doodling in your notebook? Are you more relaxed when you exercise? These are clues. Most people get stuck and stay stuck because they're waiting for someone to tell them exactly what to do. They want a clear message written in the sky.

There are clues telling you what to do, but they are small and easy to miss unless you practice staying in the moment. I went from being a lawyer to being a freelance copywriter because I kept seeing people talking about freelance writing online. I enjoyed reading about the mechanics of building a business and learning about the art and science of copywriting. There was never one lightbulb moment. I just noticed that I kept noticing freelance writing opportunities. Then one day, I decided to take one of those opportunities. That choice changed my life, but I didn't know my life had changed for more than a year afterward.

By noticing what I noticed, I had forgotten to feel stuck. I was too busy doing things. Are you waiting for motivation to do something? Then I have some bad news for you. Motivation isn't magic. Motivation comes from the neurotransmitter dopamine. Do you know what increases dopamine in your brain? Doing things.

You get motivation from doing things. You don't do things because of motivation. As someone with ADHD, and therefore a very complex relationship with dopamine, that seems incredibly unfair. When you're stuck, you need to build up enough momentum to get moving. You need to reach escape velocity. Instead of waiting for motivation to do some big thing, start doing very small things. Building escape velocity is a combination of the concepts of atomic habits and habit stacking.

You start taking a series of small actions that all feed into each other. When I get stuck on a book project, I do not decide to focus on finishing a chapter. I don't even try to focus on finishing a page. Instead, I create one notecard a day. That notecard may have one sentence or one paragraph. It might have a crude sketch for a comic. Once I do this for a few days, I feel moved to put some of those cards into a page or two.

Even on days when I can't bring myself to do a page, I keep making the cards. Many cards will never be used. Some of the cards will be useful in other ways. But the practice of making the cards helps me build the escape velocity I need to get unstuck. Remember, right now you don't need a direction, you just need movement. String together two or three very small habits to get some dopamine flowing. It might be doing one sit-up and writing one sentence. No action is too small.

Most likely, you are hyper-focused on figuring out what you

want to do. What if you stopped worrying about what you want to do with your life and instead asked, "Who do I want to be?" You have some sense of the kind of person you want to be. Just practice being that kind of person.

You know what it means to be a good person. You know what the kind of person you hope to be looks like. Instead of trying to find your calling, practice being the person you imagine you want to be. The best way to change who you are is to practice being someone else. This isn't just fake it until you make it. You have to think hard about the kind of person you want to be, and notice what kinds of things that person would do. Then you do those things.

Do you want to be someone who gets up early? Practice living that way. What do people who get up early do differently from you? They don't just will themselves out of bed. They have a system. They probably go to bed early. They also probably have good sleep hygiene. That means they get up and go to bed at the same time each day. They don't drink a lot of caffeine late in the day. They stay off their phones after a certain time. In other words, there's a lot that goes into the simple act of getting up early. If you want that trait for yourself, you can't just set your alarm earlier. This is a recipe for failure. Instead, you have to practice the habits that early-morning people have.

You don't need to do them all at once. That's another way to quickly fail. Practice one habit, develop one system at a time. Don't get mad at yourself for falling short—you're still practicing. If you put in enough repetition, if you practice long enough, you will change who you are. Practice being the person you want to be; that's all any successful person does.

Life is not going to go the way you planned. That's life. You can either get angry about the detours you are forced to go on, or you can enjoy the scenery. Often, getting unstuck only requires a change of perspective. Perhaps, you are not lost at all. Maybe whatever happened to take you off track has put you exactly where you need to be. Look for the best parts of your life, and enjoy them. The more you look for the good, the more you will find. If nothing else, life's detours give you wonderful stories to tell.

When I was a young father, being the primary caregiver to four young kids, at times, felt like a Sisyphean hellscape. Every day, there were more dishes and more laundry. These beautiful kids needed to have meals made for them three times a day, every day. It never ended. I loved caring for my children. I loved being with them all day. I did not love the drudgery. One day during lunchtime, something happened. I created a character. I became a French chef named Xavier. I started speaking to my children in a thick French accent and narrating my tasks like I was on a cooking show as I made them their summer lunch. I diced their cheese sticks and carefully folded their cold cuts like I was plating food at a Michelin-starred restaurant. The kids loved it, and I loved it too. I embraced the mundane and spiced it up with the imaginary. After that, everything from dishes to laundry became easier. It was less about drudgery and more about finding the magic in the mundane. My situation had not changed, but my attitude had. I was no longer stuck in the rut of never-ending housework. I was enjoying the small moments of life.

You may not have noticed yet, but you usually plan to get way more done in a day than is possible. It's not just you. By default, all of us overestimate what we can get done in a day and underestimate what we can get done in a year.

Life is a game of inches, not miles. Slow, plodding progress is how big projects are completed. If you fall short on what you wanted to accomplish today, the worst thing you can do is beat yourself up and resolve to work twice as hard tomorrow. When you are stuck in life, the temptation is to try to make some grand, impossible-to-accomplish plan for each day. This usually leads to more frustration. Remind yourself that something is always better than nothing. Instead of trying to write an entire article in a day, be happy with just getting an outline done. Some days you might find yourself crossing off every item on your to-do list. But most days, you only get a handful of things finished. That's a win.

If you find yourself at the end of a day where you did not do anything you wanted, spend five minutes and do a little bit towards one goal. Something is better than nothing. Those five minutes put you ahead for tomorrow and allow you to go to bed knowing you're a little closer to your goals.

Have you ever spent hours looking for something, only to find it when you stopped looking? Getting unstuck is often like that. You only make progress when you stop trying to make progress.

You don't need to make drastic changes at first. Find something you love doing. This passion needs to be independent of money, your religion, and your family. You need a hobby that brings you joy.

Your passion doesn't have to be complex or expensive. It works best if it's neither of those things. If you regularly do something you are passionate about, that passion will start to leak into other areas of your life.

You will naturally start to have more patience with things that used to frustrate you, because you have an outlet. One of my passions is collage art in my notebook. I love cutting and pasting stuff. There's no way to monetize this. I make these collages for my own pleasure. This helps me relax and gives me more creative energy for the work I do that pays me. Often, the solutions to tough work problems come to me right after I finish gluing down the final scrap of paper, even though I was not thinking about anything but the collage.

Passions and hobbies allow you to get into a kind of trance where your conscious mind is able to rest. It puts you into a creative zone where your intuition is easier to access. Plus, spending time doing things without caring about money or the opinions of others is good for your soul. When you are in the zone, the rest of the world melts away, at least for a few minutes. When you come out of your trance, you will feel more rested, and you will have more energy for getting unstuck. You might even find that after a few weeks of indulging in a passion, you aren't stuck anymore.

No matter what you are going through right now, the feelings you are dealing with are not permanent. Life will change. You will not be stuck where you are forever. One way or another, your life will change. If you want to get unstuck faster, you need to instigate some kind of change yourself. Even the smallest change can change your world.

Chapter 25

How to Create a Life You Love

When I was working as an attorney, I threw up almost every day before work. So many mornings, I would vomit in the sink and then look at myself in the mirror. I looked awful. I was miserable. My career path was slowly killing me.

That life was another lifetime ago. I closed the doors of my small law firm more than thirteen years ago. These days, I wake up excited. I sing in the shower. I annoy my teenagers with my energy getting ready for the day, and I'm not even a morning person.

I have built a life I love, not through manifestation or magical thinking. I have built my current life through trial-and-error. Happiness doesn't come from vision boards or birthday wishes. Happiness comes from intentionally creating a life you love. It comes from taking responsibility for your life.

While I don't believe in magical thinking or manifesting, I do believe our brains have far more power than we understand. But changing anything in your life requires you to take action, not just vibes. It requires you to take responsibility.

Bad things happen. Sometimes those things are your fault, and sometimes they're not. Often, things happen to you because of complex systems you have no control over or voice in. However, if you want a life filled with joy, you have to take responsibility for all of it. What happens to you may not be your fault, but it is your responsibility. The only alternative is to live life as a permanent victim of your circumstances.

Taking responsibility doesn't mean trying to control everything. Much of what happens to you, maybe most of what happens, is beyond your control. If you want to be miserable, spend all of your time trying to control everything. Taking responsibility means taking charge of solving your problems without worrying about who is to blame.

I have some mental health issues, including an anxiety disorder. It's not my fault that I have an anxiety disorder, but it's my responsibility to deal with it. Taking responsibility has meant working with therapists and doctors. It has meant developing coping mechanisms. I take long daily walks because it helps regulate my nervous system, and it allows me to manage my mental health without medication, for now.

Last year, my main source of income, freelance writing, was under serious threat. In one week, I lost three clients to AI. My contacts for two of the clients told me AI was cheaper, and even though my work outperformed AI, the price difference was so steep that their bosses wanted to eliminate all freelancers and internal marketing team members.

In that case, the problem was partly my fault. I had gotten lazy and let those three clients believe that all I did was write for them, making me easy to replace.

I took responsibility and retooled that part of my business. Today, freelancing is more profitable than ever for me. I love working with my clients, and I've taken the time to make the way I freelance AI-proof.

. . .

What can you control?

You cannot control much in this world. Technological advancements, political upheaval, and natural disasters are all outside your control.

But if you adopt a posture of radical responsibility, you will find you can always control three things. You can control your attitude, your effort, and you can choose to love. With a good attitude and a willingness to work through hard things, you can build a life that you love.

Attitude

The first step is to control your attitude. Emotions are complicated, especially if you have a mental illness. Even though I live with anxiety, I can still control my attitude. It isn't easy. Everything from social media to my own broken brain is pulling on my emotions, trying to get me to freak out, become enraged, or get discouraged.

Learning to be calm doesn't mean becoming a robot. You're allowed to feel your feelings. You should feel upset when you go through upsetting things. But it's up to you to learn how to get back to a state of calm. You cannot make good decisions when you're upset. The more you practice calmness, the easier it becomes.

After years of trying to stay calm and focused on the present, I have learned to stabilize my mood. I still have anxiety attacks from time to time. My anxiety still gets the better of me, but I have learned how to have a better attitude even while I'm a puddle of anxiety.

If you want to love your life, you have to be the kind of person you want to be around. Complaining about everything that is going wrong will not change your circumstances. It won't even make you feel better. Chronic complaining is a form of self-sabotage. It's the opposite of taking radical responsibility for your life.

When you are annoyed with something, instead of complaining, you should ask yourself if it is under your control. If you can change whatever is annoying you, put your energy towards fixing the problem instead of complaining.

If you cannot change what is annoying you, you need to let go of your frustration, accept the situation for what it is, and move on to making other areas of your life better.

Building a life you love isn't about being happy all the time. It's about deciding what you allow to influence your mood and direction.

Choose someone to serve

It is up to you to create a life you love; nobody else can do it for you. But you also cannot create a life you love on your own. I'm an introvert. I consider myself a happy hermit. But even I need other people to help create the life I love. The good news is that this doesn't mean being in a relationship. You can create a life you love if you're single, married, divorced, living with someone else, or living with several other people. The key isn't your relationship status. The key is finding someone to serve.

You cannot create a life you love by being selfish all the time. You need one or more people you love to serve. This means you do something for someone without remuneration and without expecting recognition. There are no rules for who you can serve—that's up to you.

A life of fulfillment requires you to give of your time and talents to make someone else's life better. Service has a way of putting your problems into perspective. It increases your sense of gratitude and allows you to build connections with other people. We are a social species. Connecting with other people helps our brains work more efficiently.

There are so many people who need your help. Service doesn't have to be anything big. You can help your elderly neighbor by taking out their garbage. You can pick up litter in a local park. Life gets better when it's not all about you.

Make mistakes and try again

If you want to create a life you love, you have to be willing to screw up. You won't get it right the first time. You probably won't get it right the tenth time. Often, we only find the right path in life because of our mistakes.

I would never have found a career as a writer and illustrator who makes poetry comics if I hadn't made a spectacular failure out of previous businesses. You can't let a few mistakes keep you from continuing to strive for a better life.

If you aren't willing to crash a few times, you'll never learn to ride a bike. If one skinned knee is going to stop you from trying, you will never experience the joy of racing downhill under your own power as the wind rushes past your face. Creating a life that you love isn't about being perfect. It's about being open and honest with yourself.

Decide you love your life

The last step is the hardest for most people. You have to consciously decide that you love your life. This is as close to magical thinking as I get. Having a good attitude makes your life more pleasant, even if it doesn't change your external circum-stances.

Most of us struggle with believing we love our life because we obsess over all of the things that are going wrong, and we obsess over all of the things we haven't done yet.

If you decide you love your life, you will find it easier to make other decisions that make your life even better. You have to decide that you have created a life you love, even if you don't like many of the past decisions you've made. This isn't fake it until you make it. This is giving up on perfectionism and choosing to love yourself.

Creating a life that you love means focusing on the present and learning that the past and the future are out of your control.

Even after you've created a life that you love, you will still have bad days. Somedays you will wake up and won't be feeling it. Somedays, someone will rear-end you because they are on their cell phone.

You get to decide if these are simple speed bumps or if they're off-ramps to a life of anger, bitterness, and frustration.

Having a life that you love is not about having a dream job, the right income, or being in a relationship. Building a life you love is about learning to be the kind of person you want to be around. It's about choosing to be someone who solves problems instead of complaining about them. I know you have what it takes to build the kind of life that fills you with joy.

What are you going to do today to start creating a life that you love?

Chapter 26

Life is Not a Solved Game

My youngest daughter and I sat next to each other in a crowded Oregon Coast chain restaurant called Pig'N Pancake, partaking in a delightful ritual: playing tic-tac-toe on the paper children's menu. She was eight at the time. After our second game ended in a cat's game, she looked up at me with a beautiful smile, missing two teeth, and said, "We're both too good at this game!"

Tic-tac-toe is what game theorists call a solved game. This means that the outcome of the game can be correctly predicted from any position, given enough information. Solved games are usually simple, turn-based games. Checkers is a solved game, but chess, with its nearly infinite combinations of moves, remains unsolved. Once upon a time, data scientists invested a massive amount of time and computer processing power into trying to solve games. Now, working in generative AI is too lucrative for most data scientists to spend resources on game theory.

Many tech titans seem driven by the belief that everything is a solvable game. They are willing to play chicken with the health of the planet based on the belief that generative AI will eventually be powerful enough to solve the climate crisis and every other problem currently facing the human race. Many in the AI community are creating a kind of religion where AI is both god and holy scripture, the ultimate source of knowledge.

A critical flaw (one of many) is that this approach assumes that all of life's mysteries are solvable given enough data and processing power. But life is not a solved, or even solvable, game. While chess has a nearly infinite number of moves, life has a truly infinite number of combinations.

Life is not meant to be solved. Contentment comes from wrestling with the mysteries of life. Life is experiential, not data-driven. Life has the most meaning, even for atheists and agnostics like me, when we embrace the ineffable nature of our existence in this vast, wondrous universe. There are many mysteries for which we can find solutions, mysteries that AI may help solve.

For example, scientists still don't know how massive baleen whales like humpback whales and gray whales manage to find their prey, some of the tiniest creatures on the planet, krill, in the vast oceans of the planet.

This is a mystery humans are capable of solving. This is something knowable. We just need more information, more data. Between scientific observation and generative AI, this is something we could figure out. Once we have this information, we might be able to take more effective actions to preserve the ecosystems these whales need to thrive, and improve the overall health of our planet's oceans. We should be actively solving these kinds of problems.

What scientists and AI cannot solve is why looking at the ocean sometimes fills humans with a bittersweet combination of wonder and clarity about our finite existence. This is the kind of mystery humans need to struggle against with the very human tools of art, poetry, and philosophy. Asking a chatbot why you feel sad when you look at the ocean will not bring you real answers or enlightenment. This part of life is not solvable with more data. Instead, you must learn how to sit still and feel your feelings. You must experience moments of confusion and discomfort to find any kind of contentment.

AI will not solve loneliness, the need for some humans to oppress and harm other humans, or how to best grieve the loss of a parent. It seems that part of being human is having an intrinsic, instinctual need to solve puzzles and having an irrepressible desire to better our circumstances.

Besides a rapacious desire to accumulate more wealth for investors and executives, this need to solve puzzles and find happiness is why humans have created generative AI. We have created a powerful tool in search of a problem to solve. The more we try to use AI to solve the mystery of human happiness, the unhappier we are sure to become. You need a sense of mystery to struggle against. You need to wonder, to feel, to fail, and to experience life.

In recent months, news outlets have been running stories about a new human malady, AI psychosis. In part, this new mental health issue is driven by AI chatbots amplifying human delusions. However, as this problem becomes more prevalent, there seems to be something else at work.

The human brain seems to kind of short-circuit when we try to replace the complexities of human connection with the "certainty" of connecting with a machine. We want answers, but we need questions. Discovering how to find and connect with a romantic partner, how to live with other humans who have different views and preferences, and how to mourn the dead while continuing to live are at the core of the game of life.

No amount of data crunching can solve these mysteries for you. There is no generative AI capable of generating a synthetic emotional connection that will replace organic human connections. In Buddy Holly's 1958 hit, *It's So Easy!*, he sings about how it seems easy to fall in love, but it really requires a level of foolishness, not wisdom, to truly fall in love. This silly pop song will get you closer to understanding the mysteries of human connection than any chat with a generative AI model.

Instead of trying to look for answers online, instead of trusting algorithms to lead you to the answers you need, you will find greater enlightenment and contentment by using generative human intelligence. Cultivate your imagination. Write in a notebook, sketch, write poetry, write fiction, make music, dance, hold hands, or walk in nature if you want to find clues to love, loss, and belonging. Engage with the art and experiences of other humans. Let AI solve solvable problems, and embrace the beauty of the unknown, the unknowable parts of being human.

Life is not a solvable game.

Chapter 27

How to Change Your Life Today

On a brilliant September Saturday, the kind of day that demands you go outside one last time before fall settles into its full gloom, I packed all four kids into our minivan and headed to my office.

I had spent the last week emptying and cleaning the space that had once housed the five-attorney law firm I had founded. I was about to default on the lease and file for bankruptcy. But before I said goodbye to the space forever, I wanted to make a happy memory with my children. I wanted to find some way to remember this chapter in my life as something other than a spectacular failure.

The office park was empty; none of the other businesses were open on Saturdays. My kids and I unloaded baskets holding rubber balls of all kinds of sizes and colors and headed into the empty shell of the law firm. Some of the balls were as big as my youngest, a rambunctious and enthusiastic two-year-old.

For the next two and a half hours, my kids, ages two, four, six, and eight, ran through the hallways screaming, laughing, and chasing bouncing balls. That day from more than thirteen years ago is still one of my favorite memories. You don't need to win the lottery or make a viral video to change your life. All you need is to tell yourself a better story.

When I took the kids to my office, I didn't know I was choosing to change my life. I was just muddling through being an unemployed dad who was now a full-time caregiver who was building a budding freelance writing business while my wife was in the middle of a deep depression that incapacitated her. Something fundamentally shifted while playing with my children that afternoon. I discovered that human brains are meaning-making machines.

One of the quirks of the human brain, and one of its greatest strengths, is that it finds order and meaning in the chaos of the universe, even in places where there is no order. This is why you see shapes in the clouds, some people see the face of Jesus in a piece of burnt toast, and why we have an insatiable need for stories. We see patterns where they don't exist and tell ourselves stories that didn't happen to make sense of the world.

That day I spent playing with my children, I was spinning a new story for myself. I was recasting a traumatic event in a new light. I was telling myself that I wasn't a failure. I was a good father, and I worked my ass off to make sure that story remained true. None of this was conscious at the time. I was just surviving. But this was also my way of taking responsibility for my life.

I would eventually find much more success as a freelance writer than I ever did as a lawyer. I would also find greater contentment in my life after leaving the cutthroat world of the law behind.

A big part of what made that transition possible was the stories I told myself about my experiences. I stopped casting myself as a victim of fate and started seeing myself as someone who had made some big mistakes, but who had also had some critical victories. I didn't let my failure become my final chapter. I used it as the inciting incident for the rest of my story. The day I changed my story was the day my life changed.

Not that everything instantly got better. There was a lot of work involved. But changing my story gave me hope, and hope is what I most needed to move forward. That time of my life often seems like it happened to someone else. It's strange that I occasionally still have nightmares about being a lawyer, but I have never once had a nightmare related to being a freelance writer, illustrator, or poet. In some ways, I still have work to do in fully accepting the changes I made to my story.

But even that first effort, that moment I decided to make my last day at the old office a wild play day for my kids and me, changed how I saw myself and my experiences. I chose to make my own adventure instead of passively following along a script someone else had written.

It's easy to feel like your life is just a series of events happening to you. But this keeps you from making the kinds of radical transformations you dream about. The truth is that the way to earn more money, lose weight, and be happier doesn't depend on the rest of the world cooperating with you.

You can start down the path to a better life right now by choosing to see life as an adventure that you are writing for yourself. Every obstacle, each disaster, is just a small part of a bigger story, one where you prevail in the end.

Every book ever written is just a series of horrible events happening to the main character until they are eventually able to learn from their mistakes and achieve some kind of transformation. Casting your life as a story isn't denying reality or faking it until you make it. It's exercising your agency to create the life you want.

My two oldest children had a series of horrible math teachers starting at the end of their elementary school years and continuing into middle school. They had zero confidence in their ability to do math. They thought they were "dumb" at math.

In high school, while most of their friends went into a more advanced math class as freshmen, they retook Algebra, the normal ninth-grade level math class, one they had struggled with in eighth grade.

In retaking this class, they both experienced a kind of math renaissance. They both were at the top of their class in math. They regained confidence in their math skills, and by the time they graduated, they were taking more advanced math than their friends who had started ahead of them.

Both of my oldest children were dual-enrolled in college during their senior years in high school, taking college-level math courses. This was inconceivable to both of them when they started high school.

What happened? Did they suddenly become smarter? No, they found their way to a better story. They both had great teachers who showed them that math wasn't an indecipherable foreign language, but a system for solving problems. Being bad at math was a story, and it was replaced with a story about being good at math.

You can use this same storytelling power to change your life today. You are not an aspiring writer; you are a writer. You are not a struggling artist; you are an artist on a quest to find your audience.

Allow pain to change you, and then change your pain

The craziest thing about the power of story is that you can use stories to change your past, present, and future. Memory is a slippery thing. Each time you recall a memory, you are changing that memory. Why not find a way to make your memories of past events serve you better? Why not tell yourself a powerful story about those events?

Instead of seeing a past trauma as something that ruined you, decide that the traumatic event was something that galvanized you into a warrior who now fights to make sure nobody else ever has to feel that way. The stories you tell yourself don't just have to recast the past. You can also shape your present and your future.

I've had the good fortune to live an interesting life. Many of the things that have happened to me were traumatic. But I have decided to use those events to power my narrative as someone who is a powerful survivor. I have decided to be indomitable. This doesn't mean that I'm bulletproof, or that horrible things don't sometimes happen to me. Instead, it means I know I will bounce back. I will find a way to keep chasing my dreams. I will not become hopeless.

This isn't toxic positivity. I feel the pain. I grieve the dead, I cry with heartbreak, but I refuse to wallow in suffering. I allow my pain to change me, and then I change my pain to suit my needs by creating a useful narrative. It all starts for me by practicing looking for stories.

Are you worried that you don't know how to change the story you tell yourself? I promise you have the power to change your story. Start by noticing what stories you are already telling yourself. What repetitive thoughts do you have? Do you call yourself stupid when you make a mistake? That's a story.

You can also practice your storytelling by looking for stories around you. Make up stories about the birds in the sky or the squirrels in the park. This is one reason I love writing haiku each day about what I see as I go about the world. It's a mindfulness practice that also exercises my storytelling muscles.

Notice how you think about others. You are not a neutral observer of the world. You are always telling yourself stories about what you observe and experience. You cannot help it. Story is how humans encode memories and interpret data. Changing your life starts with taking control of the stories you tell. Changing your story starts with noticing how many stories you already believe and then writing new stories to better serve you.

So much of the advice you see in self-help books is about noticing your story and being mindful about the stories you tell. It's about deciding to chart your own course instead of relying on autopilot. Never stop examining the stories you tell yourself

Most of the stories you tell yourself have a useful shelf life. Since I was the oldest child with three siblings and two often-neglectful parents, I've always seen myself as a caregiver who must put the needs of others before myself.

This helped me as a child, and served me reasonably well when my children were younger. But my children are now twenty-one, nineteen, seventeen, and fifteen. I needed to allow them to grow up.

FROM THE UNKEMPT FIELD,

CRICKET CONVERSATIONS FLOAT

THROUGH OPEN WINDOWS

. . .

I've had to work on letting go of that old story and learn how to prioritize my own needs and allow my children to be in charge of their own lives. I'm now weaving a new story about being more of an on-call consultant to my children and less of their caregiver. I will always be their dad, but their needs and my needs have changed.

You will never arrive at the place you want to be in life. Life is an endless cycle of reinvention and reinterpretation. That's the beauty of being human. That is the redeeming value of suffering. Our capacity for love opens us up to a degree of suffering that connects us to every other human being.

What you choose to do with that suffering is up to you. You can horde it, wallow in misery, or you can use the power of story to transform suffering into a way to help and connect with other human beings, bringing more joy into your life. The choice is always yours.

What story are you going to tell yourself today?

Chapter 28

Be a Sea Turtle

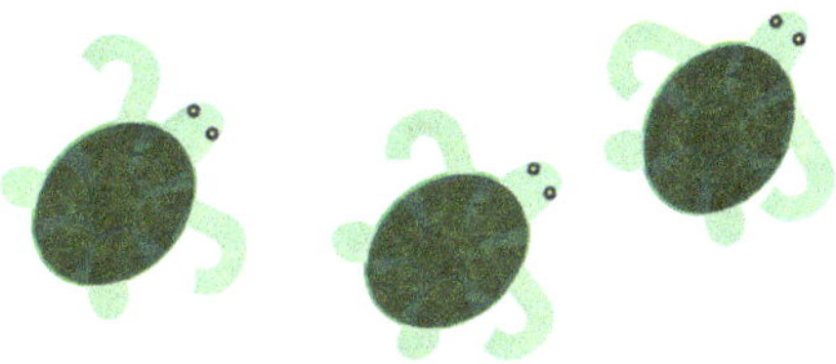

Before finding success and happiness as a writer and illustrator, I crawled from failure to failure. I thought I was following the plan. I graduated from college, attended law school, and opened my own law firm. I was miserable.

My law practice eventually imploded, and I walked away from my legal career to become a copywriter. Life was better, but something was still missing. I hadn't found my element. Once I discovered I had a knack for combining compelling visuals and words, it transformed everything about my life.

Visual storytelling was my element. It made my copywriting and content writing more interesting and allowed me to explore any topic I was curious about. After years of slow progress, I suddenly felt like I was gliding.

I was like a sea turtle.

One of the great ironies of life is that one of the ocean's most graceful creatures begins life on land. Sea turtles are slow, awkward, lumbering things on the sand.

Every inch of progress is the result of a fierce triumph of will.

All of nature seems to scream, "You can't do this. You are not built for this place."

The sea turtle seems to reply, "I am doing this."

Hatchlings look ridiculous as they scamper in a mad dash for life from their broken shells to the safety of the sea.

Once in the water, sea turtles transform into graceful, agile, fast beings. They move with the combined grace of a ballerina and the precision of a jet fighter. If sea turtles lumber on land, they fly through the water.

For most of my life, I felt like a marooned sea turtle. Every move felt wrong. There was a mismatch between my skills, inclinations, and my environment. I did my best to adapt. But every accomplishment was hard won. Nothing ever felt easy or natural.

Circumstances eventually drove me from the beach and into the ocean. I was scared to leave the familiar, rugged, harsh terrain I had known all my life. Then the moment came when I hit the water, and I glided forward with an astonishing speed and grace.

Like the sea turtle, I was not built for the place I was born.

The rules and norms that seemed to work for everyone else stifled me. Working a regular job for four decades sounded like torture, and my every attempt to live that way eroded my spirit.

Life in the ocean remains perilous for sea turtles, but their bodies are better adapted to evading and outmaneuvering ocean predators than they are to land predators.

As fast as turtles can swim, on the longest leg of their migration, they get a boost from their environment—the East Australian Current (EAC) carries turtles swiftly across the ocean.

After years of writing, I still felt something was missing. I was happy to be off the beach, but I was looking for a current.

I found my own version of the EAC. Comics allowed me to enter a flow. This medium used all my skills and encompassed all of my interests. It gave me the freedom to be myself.

Most of us go through phases where we feel like a sea creature trapped on land. Imagine if we judged sea turtles only by what they can do on land. But that's exactly what we do to ourselves. Our purpose in life isn't to settle for a life of drudgery and difficulty. Your purpose is to find your element. You may be scrambling and struggling now, but that is only because you are driven by instinct to pull yourself towards the place where you belong.

You are destined to find the element through which you can soar.

There is a place for you in the world. You have skills and abilities that are perfectly suited for something. If you feel like a turtle stuck on land, you need to keep experimenting. You need to remain curious.

You may find that your parents, teachers, and gurus don't have the answers for you. You may need to go into the wild and find your own way.

If you're unsure what excites you, spend time with people who are passionate about what they do. It could be knitting or marginalia from medieval manuscripts. Spending time with passionate people is inspiring.

One of my favorite newsletters is Emily Nunn's *The Department of Salad*. *The Department of Salad*. I subscribed not because I have any special love of salads, but because Emily is so passionate about salads. Her enthusiasm is contagious. One of the great joys of life is watching people share what lights them up. *The Department of Salad* helps give me the courage to keep making the kind of work that excites me.

For most of their lives, sea turtles move in large groups. They gain strength by being part of a group. You may have to find your own way to your passion, but you do not have to spend your entire life alone. You may find it easier to find joy in life by becoming a part of a community.

Whatever your struggles are, just know that there is a place for you. You will find your way to the sea, as long as you keep moving.

Chapter 29

What Do We Owe the Dead?

There is a graveyard deep in rural Southeast Idaho, behind a Mormon church, where more than half of the gravestones bear my last name. I'm directly related to all the McBrides in that graveyard and most of the other people interred there with different surnames. One of those gravestones marks the final resting place of my parents, and on that grave marker, despite my objections, is carved my name, along with those of my three siblings.

I've only been to that graveyard two times, and both times it was pouring rain, something unusual for a place on the edge of the Great Basin, America's largest desert. Neither of those visits was for the funerals of my parents; I skipped those services.

I lived most of my life as part of a faith tradition that made doing work for the dead a central tenet of not only religion but of life. In Mormonism, you exist as a link in an eternal chain connecting your descendants to your ancestors and to God. It was taken for granted that we all have souls, or spirits, that will continue to exist after we have sloughed off this mortal coil. In Mormonism, the dead are always watching you.

I come from pioneer stock. My McBrides immigrated from England, crossed the plains at the literal cost of life and limb. My ancestors were some of the first white settlers in what still looks to be the godforsaken land of Southeast Idaho.

Being faithful to God means obeying the leaders of the Church and refraining from doing anything that would dishonor the sacrifices of your ancestors. As a boy, I felt the constant pressure of God, my parents, my church leaders, and my long-dead ancestors pressing down on me. My life choices didn't feel like my own. Even mundane decisions carried the impossible weight of eternal expectations.

I was taught that we had a serious responsibility toward the living and the dead. If we failed either the living or the dead, we put their eternal salvation, as well as our own, at risk. When I turned 19, I served a two-year mission for my Church in Taiwan, where I would preach about this responsibility, among other things. I was doing my part for the living. My kindred dead were always watching me.

The most common religious practice in Taiwan involves something many Westerners sneeringly call ancestor worship. It's immediately obvious to anyone who takes the time to learn about these practices that the people do not worship their dead ancestors. They honor them, and they believed in caring for them—not that different from what I had been taught and what I was then teaching.

In Taiwan and in much of East Asia, many people believe that the dead, or ghosts, inhabit a realm close to ours where they cannot get the essentials they need unless their descendants provide for them. This involved burning images of clothing and money. It sometimes involved putting incense sticks in food to allow the ancestors to eat the spirit of the food. Life as a devout Mormon, and as an honorable Taiwanese son or daughter, revolves around taking care of the responsibilities owed to dead ancestors. Responsibilities that never ended.

I've arrived at middle-middle age. During my journey, I have accumulated a lot of honored dead. What do I owe these friends and family members? I no longer believe that I am responsible for their salvation. I'm open to the idea of each of us having some kind of soul, but I'm not clear on the specifics. I'm also not sure how much contact we mortals can have with the deceased. Are ghosts and spirits real? I'm not willing to bet against it. But there's one thing I am confident of. The only debt or responsibility we owe the dead is to live our lives to the fullest.

What do my dead parents want from me? What does my recently deceased father-in-law want? Surely, if they want anything, it is for me to love their grandchildren deeply and to live a life of happiness and peace. They cannot hug their grandchildren, so I will give my children extra hugs for them. They can no longer feel the wind whip their cheeks as it comes off the ocean, and so I will experience that as often as I can.

I do not know what eternity is like. None of us does. We all have our beliefs, often supported by our experiences, desires, and sometimes even our studies. However, like the humble atom is the building block of all matter, single, discrete moments are the building blocks of eternity. If you want to build a happy forever after, you must fully live as many moments of tiny joy in the present as possible.

I still feel awe at the sight of an eagle diving to snatch a fish out of the river. I stop and examine the colors of a beetle crossing my path and am stunned by the gorgeous purple and blue hues of its exoskeleton. I stop and watch as the sun sets in the west, and my children and I laugh at each other's jokes every day. I do these things for myself in the present because I am not living for the dead. Instead of worrying about my ancestors, I'm thinking about my descendants. I am living for my children and my eventual grandchildren. I'm creating a legacy of joy and mindfulness. My children know I am here for them. Two of my children are adults, and the other two are high schoolers. My gift for them is to release them from any pressure to live their lives in ways that please me or our army of dead ancestors. I know that the best thing I can do for all of my descendants is to heal my generational trauma and to live life moment to moment.

I have a project that I occasionally work on that explores the tension between grief and hope. I don't know that the full project will ever see the light of day because my work on it is so plodding, and it feels too raw still, even after six years.

Grief is a critical part of the human experience. You cannot lose someone you love, no matter what your religious beliefs are, and not be affected. When we deny the reality of a loss, we lose some part of our humanity. However, to be consumed with grief without ever allowing it to fade is to live a diminished life, shackled to the memory of someone who cannot offer comfort or guidance. I know a few widows and widowers who agonize over every life choice after the death of a spouse, trying to divine what their spouse would've wanted. That is no way to live.

A part of the grieving process must be choosing to step fully into the present moment of this life, living for yourself, and those who are still here. You cannot live for your ancestors.

I once took several of my children to see the Broadway musical *Hadestown*. This musical is based on the ancient Greek tragedy Orpheus and Eurydice, and it relates perfectly to the tension between grief and hope. It may seem strange that seeing a musical where the main characters fail because of a combination of their choices and circumstances far beyond their control could make you feel more hope for the world, but it does. One of the show's themes is that we must sing sad songs all the way through, even though we already know how they will end. We do this because we are human. The catharsis and pathos you go through watching and listening to tragic works like this give you the strength to keep battling.

We need all kinds of art in our troubled world. Silly and happy stories help lift our spirits and distract us. But sad stories are needed too. These help us remember that we are human and that suffering is a part of our existence. These tragic tales elevate us; they increase our empathy and reconnect us to our humanity.

Hadestown is also about the cycle of the seasons. Spring always follows winter. Orpheus loses Eurydice in the winter, and at the end of the show, it is spring again. Life is celebrated even though the losses of winter are still fresh. We sing the sad songs all the way through so we can continue to move forward, taking the memories of our lost loved ones with us without chaining ourselves to the place in time where they fell.

There is a story in the New Testament when Jesus's friend Lazarus dies. Lazarus's sisters, Mary and Martha, are deep in grief. Jesus, the Son of God, then does something remarkable.

Jesus wept.
—John 11:35

After mourning the loss of his friend and comforting Mary and Martha, Jesus raises Lazarus from the dead. Even after the loss of my faith, I've always found this story deeply moving and puzzling. Jesus knew he was going to bring Lazarus back from the dead, so why bother weeping? Was it performative? I'm not a biblical scholar, but I interpret this story to mean that Jesus was so full of compassion for Mary and Martha that he was moved to tears at their grief, he shared that grief, and then he went back to doing his work. He sang the sad song all the way through. I still weep for the dead. But then I dry my tears and get back to the work of living.

I was born in Southeast Idaho, but I will not be buried there. I refuse this legacy of my ancestors. They are dead, but I will continue to live so that my children, my descendants, can live a freer life, unbound by my wishes or the oppressive, moldering desires of their ancestors.

Chapter 30

Walk in the Rain

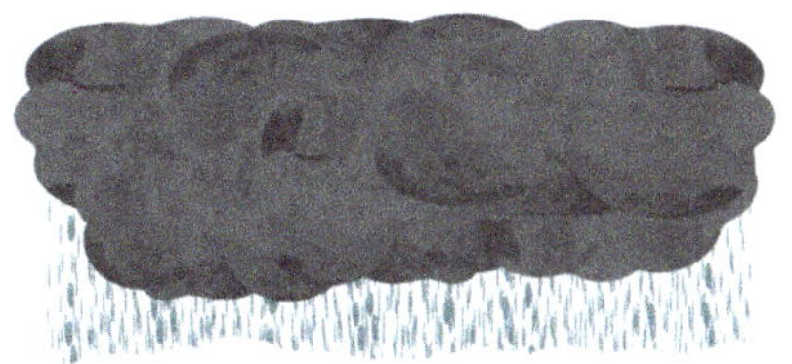

My favorite thing about Oregonians is that we almost never use umbrellas. This is kind of a strange thing since in Western Oregon, it rains almost every day from the middle of October through the middle of April. But it's a source of pride for us. We would rather get a little wet than have to worry about carrying around one more thing.

Comfort is overrated. In life, you have to choose between being comfortable and being interesting. I chose to pursue an interesting life, and that has meant I have taken a lot of walks in the rain. Walking in the rain is an intentional activity for me. I love grabbing my jacket and mud boots and heading out onto rainy trails because I know I will have nature to myself. There is something glorious about seeing the raindrops fall through the leaves and onto the ground, creating fresh, temporary ecosystems with hundreds of tiny puddles.

I sometimes stand and watch rain splash down on the river and lose all sense of time. Between the flow of the river and the pitter-pat-pat of the rain, I fall into a trance while the water carries away all of my stress and anxiety. It's better than any meditation app or psychotropic drug.

Mindfulness comes in many forms. Standard meditation practices don't work for me. But walking in a good, strong rainstorm quiets my mind and allows me to be in the present, without judgment.

However, it's not all bliss. When the rain is especially fierce, it starts to soak my jeans and penetrate my all-weather boots. My socks get soaked, and a sense of cold will sometimes snap me out of the spell I've fallen under.

It's then that I usually return to the car, change my clothes if I was smart enough to remember to bring a spare set, or I crank up the car heater and dry out while writing poetry in my notebook and jotting down what I noticed during my rain walk.

SIT, MESMERIZED BY
SERIES OF RAINDROP RIPPLES,
WATER RUNS OFF COAT

While it's impossible to quantify, I'm certain that I write my best poetry after having been out in the elements long enough to be deeply uncomfortable.

So often in life, we miss out on great stories and life-altering experiences because we are afraid of being uncomfortable. We avoid trying new things out of fear of looking stupid, and we dodge any challenges that might require us to ask someone else for help. We fail to pitch magazines because we are scared of being rejected. We confuse comfort for safety and refuse to take any risks.

Life gets better when you learn to be content with discomfort. No matter how many daring things you do, you will never fully outrun fear. That feeling you get in your stomach when things get scary can either be your signal to push through, or it can be your excuse to back out.

Bruce Springsteen still gets stage fright more than 50 years into his music career. But he sees that anxiety as a good omen. It means he still cares about the work. He is content with that discomfort. Being uncomfortable is not the same as being unsafe. The sooner you learn to distinguish between comfort and safety, the sooner your life will become more interesting.

I have been self-employed my entire adult life. I have lots of great stories. I've been shot at while driving down a highway in San Jose, California, on my way to pass out flyers for a low-flush toilet company, closed a deal to license an illustration for a book cover while playing in the snow with my kids, and written sales copy while watching the sun slink behind the Pacific Ocean from a seaside coffee shop.

Behind every great story, there are years of muddling and floundering. I have had to endure a lot of emotional discomfort as I've blazed a trail in search of an unconventional life. However, I have also done things most people only ever dream of.

Perhaps the hardest thing about living an interesting life is the constant questioning of your choices by extended family members who think you should settle down and live a normal life. But I don't want to settle in any sense of the word.

I've learned to be content not knowing what will happen next. The truth is nobody knows the future. Being human is living moment to moment. I've seen family members lose secure jobs and watched friends travel through South America while freelancing for a summer.

You are only promised this moment. Don't live in fear of a future that may never come, and don't fall in love with a future that might fall through. Focus on what is happening around you right now because now is the time for living.

You don't have to be self-employed to live an interesting life, though it does help. You also don't have to be an artist to live an interesting life. However, you cannot be an artist if you always choose comfort over adventure. Art is made from stories, and the most interesting stories start when things go wrong.

The key to living an interesting life is to challenge yourself to do things you're scared of. Discomfort comes in many shapes and sizes, but emotionally it's always rooted in fear. That is why it's so easy to mistake discomfort for danger. Our lizard brains would much rather we never change anything.

An interesting life happens when you take the stairs instead of the elevator, when you make small talk with the person behind you in line at the grocery store, and when you choose to wear the fedora instead of the baseball cap.

If you're paying attention, life will give you plenty of opportunities to do the interesting thing. The question is, are you willing to get a little wet, or are you going to cling to your umbrella when it starts to rain? When you choose to walk in the rain, the world comes alive in a new way. Rainstorms are when the frogs and snails come out. It's also when insights and ideas usually show up.

You are free to settle for a normal life. But if you sometimes hear a voice telling you there is more to life than dry socks and spreadsheets, you might be happier living an interesting life. You'll never know until you let go of being comfortable and dare to take a walk in the rain. I'll be out jumping in puddles, waiting for you!

Chapter 31

The Messy Business of Changing Your Life

I parked my blue minivan, holding all of the detritus left behind by four school-age kids, in the far corner of the Walmart parking lot on a Tuesday afternoon, putting as much distance between me and any other car as possible, turned up The Cure's *Just Like Heaven*, and screamed as loud and for as long as my lung capacity would allow. Then I put my head down on the steering wheel, closed my eyes, and sobbed.

There's something about the way Robert Smith always sounds like he's crying while singing his beautiful, haunting melodies that gives me permission to feel the full weight of my angst.

After my playlist ended, I put the car in drive, parked closer to the doors, and went inside to complete my errands, temporarily relieved of some of the pressure I had buckled under twenty minutes earlier.

One of the biggest lies we tell ourselves is that life and time are straight lines. But life is full of curves, switchbacks, and steep drop-offs. Not every minute is equal. Some minutes last for weeks while others pass in the blink of an eye. That day in the minivan, one of the many times I've engaged in primal scream therapy, was an especially long one. My life was a mess. I was failing and flailing. I was also in the middle of a major life transformation. I didn't realize it, but at that moment, I was caught. No longer a caterpillar, but not yet a butterfly.

One of the most disturbing things I've ever learned is what really happens inside a chrysalis. Like millions of children, my kids had watched caterpillars feed for weeks and then build cocoons in a soft net-like cage, and later emerge as butterflies that they released into the sky. Caterpillars are not just sprouting wings inside those opaque organic structures. Before a caterpillar can transform into a butterfly or moth, it must first completely melt down. Literally. If you were to crack open a chrysalis in the middle of the process, you would find it filled with a soupy goo. Metamorphosis is a messy process.

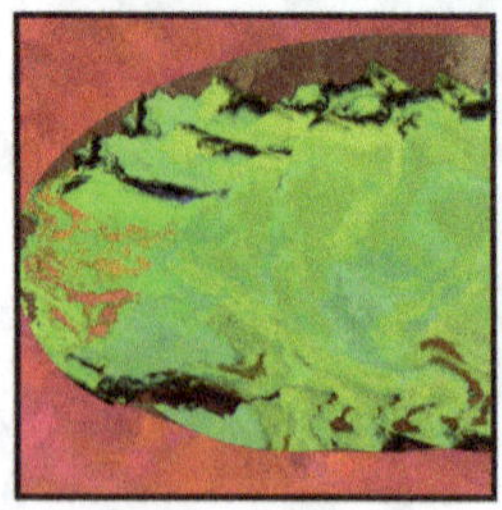

Personal transformation is not clean or clinical. Decades of self-help literature and influencers have convinced us that changing your life is just a matter of following a few carefully defined steps. Listening to a podcast or reading a *New York Times* best-selling book by an attractive, B-tier celebrity author makes changing your life seem simple. It's as easy as changing your shirt. What could be more straightforward than following a five, or seven, or twenty-step process?

But just as you can never step in the same river twice, no two humans can ever walk the same trail in life. What works for someone else may not work for you, at least not without some adaptation. Humans are evolutionarily built to resist change until it is absolutely necessary. It's not just addicts that often have to hit rock bottom before making the life changes required to thrive, and not just survive. Most of us must first experience burnout before we can summon the willpower to overhaul our toxic habits and thought patterns. And once you are ready to change, not only will change be tough, but it will be uneven.

At first, you will miss more days of workouts than you will complete. You will keep drinking soda for weeks after resolving to stop. You will keep being mean to yourself, even after you have been converted to the power of positive self-talk. These are not failures. These are the messy parts of the self-transformation process that often get left out of all the glossy self-help books and perfectly edited podcasts.

For me, the hardest part of changing my life wasn't all the ways I was falling short. The hardest part, the most painful part, was trying to hold onto my past identity while working on becoming something else entirely. I wanted to be both a caterpillar and a butterfly. But I was neither. I was a puddle of slime. Before you can transform your life, you first have to have a meltdown.

The reason most people stay stuck in lives they are ambivalent about at best is that change is hard and painful. We all want to grow wings and soar, but most of us are reasonably comfortable being cute caterpillars, and the thought of having to melt down that identity of the caterpillar and form a new one as a butterfly is too messy. What would your family say?

All those years ago, in the messy, blue minivan, parked in the far corner of the parking lot, I was yearning to be an artist. I knew I had something different inside of me, something that had to come out. But I had grown up in a household where being any kind of creative was seen as a sure path to poverty. Art was only barely tolerated as a hobby. But art as a vocation was unthinkable.

One of the first things I ever heard from my in-laws, before I married their daughter, was the two of them ridiculing the craftsman who had built a fancy gazebo in their backyard for their older son's wedding. That craftsman was a joke because he had an advanced degree in Japanese literature and was now a lowly gazebo maker. My fiancée even joked that she was maying me for my F.E.P. (future earning potential). I was on track to go to law school and be a lawyer.

While Robert Smith sang and tears rolled down my cheeks, I was really mourning because I knew the path I had to take meant I was going to be rejected by everyone I knew. I was melting down my identity as a serious, smart person, a lawyer, and figuring out how to form a new identity. None of this was conscious. I was just having a meltdown.

More than a decade later, things are much clearer. My parents would die never seeing me fully emerge as my true artist self, but with a grudging acceptance that I was happier not being a lawyer. My in-laws only grew firmer in their resentment over my choices and more convinced by every success that I was failing. My relationship with my wife never recovered. However, from that gooey mess in the minivan, I eventually emerged with wings. Perhaps more moth than butterfly, but soaring nonetheless.

I'm now comfortable telling strangers that I'm a poet-cartoonist, something that's not even adjacent to a real job. I've worked hard to figure out a way to make money from my art. And while my art doesn't yet 100% support me, I still make about half my income from freelancing for businesses, I do live life on my own terms.

I don't have a real job, probably never will again, and I love that! Even my freelance work for companies draws on my creativity and allows me to make a living from my way of living instead of just working so that I can stay alive one more day. I have made wonderfully supportive and creative friends both locally and across the globe. I'm part of a community of creative weirdos.

Most importantly, my life choices have given my children permission to dream of unconventional lives. They feel more freedom as teenagers and young adults to live life as their true selves than I ever did at their ages. They are already discovering in their teens and twenties the secrets I only learned in my forties.

For me, getting gooey meant understanding that to live a life of contentment, I needed a way to make enough money so I could "buy" time to make art. It meant accepting that I was weird. I am an artist, and denying that fact only makes life harder for me.

Sometimes I think about the Japanese literature scholar who made gazebos in the summer for pompous jerks in the Bay Area. I bet they made a lot of money, getting to work outdoors and with their hands, and had much less stress than the doctors, lawyers, engineers, and executives they were working for. I hope they also had plenty of time to read Japanese literature and share their nerdy joy with other like minded nerds.

Eric Carle's book *The Very Hungry Caterpillar* is one of the most famous children's books of all time. When most schoolchildren have their first experience with a class set of caterpillars-turned-butterflies, the unit starts with a reading of this book. Carle's book ends with the creature emerging as a butterfly from the chrysalis and flying away. He skips the part of the process where the caterpillar melts into a pile of goo; it is a children's book after all. He also skips the part that happens after the butterfly emerges and flies away. The butterfly still has to continue to live.

Accepting that I wanted to be an artist and then working to become an artist was the most painful process in my life. I'm still struggling with the emotions and fallout from this massive shift in my life. However, the story didn't end when I licensed my first illustration for a book cover, or when I published my first, or my sixth, book.

Each day I wake up to a mix of rejection emails, requests for revisions, and, when I'm lucky, an acceptance of a pitch. I am a different person, a different creature, from the man in the minivan, screaming. But I'm not done growing or changing.

This is where the analogy of the caterpillar and the butterfly (or moth in my case) wears a little thin. You and I have no final form. I'm still growing and learning. I will be fifty next year, and I'm still learning new things about the way my brain works and what makes my soul thrive every day.

I've only come this far on my journey because I didn't quit when things got messy. I refused to fail. Every time I fell, screwed up, or was rejected was just another beat in my story. I refused to let any momentary failure be the end of my tale. Success in life isn't about success; it's just a stubborn refusal to concede defeat. I never made any "30 under 30" lists of successful, influential people, and am not likely to make any "50 under 50" list either. Hell, I may not even ever be able to retire.

Plenty of people who think they know me well look at my life and think I'm a failure. Every day I choose to keep moving forward, to keep learning and trying new things. However, now, instead of walking from place to place like a caterpillar, I flutter my awkward wings and fly.

While I still find screaming at the top of my voice in my car in a deserted parking lot to be cathartic, I find I rarely need that outlet anymore. I'm finally comfortable with the phase of life I'm in, and the creature I am.

If you're in the middle of a meltdown, if you feel like your life is a pile of goo, take heart. You are in the middle of a metamorphosis. It's messy and often ugly, but you are undergoing a necessary phase change. Keep pushing through this, and one day you will find yourself flying off into the sky in search of new adventures.

IN SUMMERTIME, WE BECAME FERAL,
DRINKING FROM HOSES, RIDING BIKES,
ENTERTAINING CUTE LIFEGUARDS,
AND RACING THE SUN HOME.
WE SUMMITED HILLS
AND STUFFED OUR MOUTHS
FULL OF GUM
WITHOUT
CARES
ABOUT
OUR SAFETY,
MELANOMA,
OR CHOLESTEROL.
WE ALL LOVED EACH OTHER
WITHOUT HAVING TO SAY IT,
AND DEBATED THE MYSTERIES:
GIRLS, PHILOSOPHY, AND DEPECHE MODE.

Chapter 32

The Luxury of Boredom

Where I grew up, none of us spent the summer at sleepaway camp or rushing between music lessons and rock climbing gyms. At best, we would get five or six days at scout camp or a family road trip. But the responsibility for filling up most summer days fell upon our slouched shoulders.

Outside of school sports, the only after-school activities the children of my community had were watching TV, hanging out with the wrong crowd, and listening to the radio. In the long, languid summers of my teenage years, the air buzzed with a single question. What are we going to do?

Our parents went to work and left us to fend for ourselves. Those of us with mothers who worked to maintain the home during the day were ushered out before noon and not welcomed back before dinner at the earliest, with the often unspoken understanding that we should only return right before sunset.

All year round, but especially in the summer, my cohort of Gen-X young men were suburban lost boys.

We had all the freedom in the world, and too often we sat around wishing it away. What a tremendous gift my generation was given. We had the luxury of boredom. At the risk of sounding like the old man who yells at the clouds, boredom is too rare in society today.

We believe boredom and tedium to be the great enemies, dulling our minds and lulling us into a sleepless stupor. But the monotony of having nothing to do is a fertile field for imagination and creativity to work their miracles.

Boredom is where creativity takes root. It is where curiosity is nourished. Crazy ideas and revolutionary experiments are hard to come by when every waking hour is filled with something. You often need the nothing space that boredom fosters to change the world. Instead of allowing our minds to wander and for ideas to ferment in the activating agent of boredom, children, teens, and adults look at their phones and swipe at the first sign of boredom. We microdose dopamine.

We have instant access to just about any song ever written, every TV show or movie ever filmed, and any video game ever produced. When most of us feel sad, lonely, confused, or bored, instead of retreating into our thoughts or imagination, we try to drink from a firehose of content and then wonder why we're still so thirsty.

Our culture of hyper-productivity doesn't help either. We are bombarded with messages from bosses and self-help gurus that we cannot waste time. Instead, we must always be working on something, listening to audiobooks on double-speed or faster, or hustling and grinding our way to riches. Writers are especially vulnerable to toxic productivity. Even though writing is thinking, and good writing requires a certain amount of staring off into space and following rabbit holes that will lead nowhere, writers feel a push to get more words down on the page, as if it's the quantity of words that matters rather than the way those words are arranged and the thoughts behind those words.

Perhaps this is why so many people are so eager to outsource creative tasks to AI. They can feel good about getting more done without any thought to the quality of the output or what kind of deranged cyborgs we are turning ourselves into when we give up a core part of our humanity—our creativity—to machines.

We would rather volunteer to donate our parts to Dr. Frankenstein so he can create his monster than come face-to-face with our true selves by being bored. We fear boredom because the only one there to meet us is our true selves.

We would rather shake our fist at the algorithms for not pushing our content than spend the necessary time being bored that great writing demands. We are more afraid of doing nothing than we are of working ourselves to death. We would rather read about mindfulness and download meditation apps than stop doing things and just watch the world move around us. The moment we start to move into a space of stillness, we freak out and decide meditation and mindfulness are not for us after all.

Boredom is the creative hack you're too sacred to use. Some of my fondest memories are of the times I spent lying on my stomach as a kid, staring at the grass in our yard. Looking at the grass up close, I noticed that each blade was unique. The mower blade cropped each blade differently, with their tops having strange angles. Not even the colors of the blades of grass were genuinely uniform. Each one had its unique pattern, like zebra stripes, only in different shades of green.

The real magic of the lawn was the world of activity happening where the grass erupted from the ground. My lawn was teeming with an ecosystem I had never before considered. I saw ants, ladybugs, spiders, aphids, crickets, grasshoppers, and dragonflies in my yard. Because I was so bored and had so little to do, I had to lie down to watch the grass grow. But I came away from all those grass-watching sessions with a creative energy. They fueled my curiosity.

I didn't understand it at the time, but being bored was what allowed me to have the capacity to learn and create. Even now, thirty or forty years later, those sessions staring at the grass inform who I am. My drive to create poetry comics and fight climate change took root in my soul when I was just a bored kid. My belief that the world is full of stories comes from my experiences staring at the individual blades of grass.

As parents, we chose not to fill our children's summer days with activities, camps, and lessons. We let them be bored. This led to some fantastic creativity. One summer, our children wrote a musical together. They all love to draw and doodle. All four of our children love music and play at least one musical instrument. When my children are bored, they lie on their beds, noodling with a guitar, keyboard, or baritone ukulele, discovering chords, and sometimes writing songs. They write poetry, sketch, and paint. I recently discovered that my youngest writes short stories in secret, like a teenage Emily Dickinson who has watched too many episodes of *Stranger Things*.

They are all still probably on their phones way too much, as am

I, but as they have grown and become adults and teenagers who are not afraid of boredom. Boredom has become a part of the background of their lives.

I still struggle against the pressure to create and share something every day. But my best work, my most interesting work, is not done under the pressure of a deadline. Instead, my best work always comes out of periods of restlessness, of boredom.

Great ideas come when we give them time to develop. Boredom is a way to rest your mind, to free up energy so desperate inputs can ferment together in strange, original ways. The annoying sound of the clock when the house is too silent, the way the woman standing in front of you in line at the grocery store smelled, and the interesting pattern of the plaster on your blank wall are all ingredients for your next creation. Whether you're a writer, musician, or visual artist, you cannot afford to be busy all of the time. Your most interesting art will emerge when you allow boredom to collide with curiosity.

Unless you are a trust-fund baby, you also have to pay the bills. The pressure to make more stuff, to get more done, is not just cultural, it's also economic. Most of us who make a living from our creativity do not have the luxury of spending a decade on what creative project, to the exclusion of everything else. However, if you're honest with yourself, you will find it's easier to rely on the crutch of productivity and produce a lot of mediocre work than it is to live with occasional boredom and uncertainty.

In the end, making a living from your writing, or any other form of creativity, does not mean choosing between quality and quantity. It's being brave enough to balance both. It means having a system that helps you generate not just ideas, but good ideas. Boredom is key to any system of human-based idea generation.

When I was a teenager, boredom was the enemy. As an adult, I came to see boredom as a luxury that I could not afford. I spent many years churning out content for myself and for my clients, never stopping to wonder if I could be making things another way. As a mature writer and artist, I understand that boredom is not a luxury at all. Boredom is a necessity. Boredom is a prerequisite for making interesting work that matters and for living a fulfilling life, a life of contentment.

Until you are willing to sit with your thoughts and stare into the soul of your true self in moments of distraction-free quiet, you will never know just how creative and powerful you are. The next time you have nothing to do, smile because you are about to embark on a key phase of the creative process.

Chapter 33

Get Out of Your Head and Into the World

My optometrist cocked her head to the side and looked at me with the same confused expression as my seven-year-old Havanese when he's trying to work out which trick I want him to do to earn a treat.

"What do you mean you're not at your desk all day? I thought you said you were a freelance writer and illustrator." She asked.

I explained that while I do spend a lot of time at my desk, that's where the least important part of my work happens.

Writing and drawing are really just types of thinking. Before I know what I think, I have to go out into the world and see what's happening. I need a lot of input before I can create any output.

"Well, because of your age and eyesight, you still need progressive lenses." She said as we completed the rest of the eye exam, giving up on understanding how a writer works without spending every second at a desk.

In a world of remote work, isolation, loneliness, cascading mental health crises, and screens everywhere from our phones to our refrigerators, it's never been more important for us to get outside. One of the most toxic things about social media is that it

211

tends to drive us further into our own minds instead of connecting us to other people. Every selfie we take, every thought we post, is first run through the social media filter in our brain. What will people think about this? Will this get a lot of likes? Will the comments and likes make me cry?

Spending too much time only thinking your thoughts is not healthy. It leads to you overanalyzing everything. It keeps you from truly living your life. There is loneliness everywhere. It has always been there. There's a broad scientific consensus that social media is making most of us lonelier. There is a lot of talk about the loneliness crisis in different groups.

The truth is, loneliness has always existed. Being lonely has always been a normal, if unpleasant, part of the human experience. But something is different now. One difference is that more and more people have decided that since their loneliness is not their fault, their loneliness isn't their responsibility either. More and more people give up, believing their problems can only be solved by someone else. This attitude, combined with a massive rise in being risk-averse to any form of rejection, leads to you getting trapped in a state of loneliness. You get used to your loneliness; it becomes your default state, a prison of your own construction.

When you feel trapped in loneliness, you stop noticing anything about the way other people feel and act, unless it directly impacts you. You eventually stop noticing much of anything that happens outside of your own head. However, just like I have to get input from the outside world to create my work, you need input from the outside world to create a better life. You have to get out of your head and head out into the world. Once you train yourself to notice what is happening on your street, or at your local park, or even just outside your window, you start to loosen the bars in your prison of loneliness and despair.

The most important work you will ever do on yourself will not come from a self-help book or even therapy. It will come when you choose to start noticing and caring about things outside of yourself. Therapy and self-help literature can only take you so far. Therapy only works if you use the tools your therapist is trying to share with you. Nothing will change about your life until you change something about your life

Life would be easier if you came home to a winning lottery ticket, or if a man in a trench coat showed up at your door with a briefcase full of cash, announcing you'd been discovered as the next star, whisking you away to your new life as a celebrity. But nobody is coming to rescue you. You may feel like a damsel in distress, but you're going to need to be your own hero.

Nothing in your life will ever change until you change something in your life. Every scientist knows that if you keep running the same tests, without ever changing any of the variables, you will keep getting the same results. But if you make even a small change, over time, you can drastically improve the results you're seeing.

CRISP WIND
ENSEMBLE,

FALL COLORS
DANCE ON
WATER

DUCKS GLIDE
ACROSS POND

You have to get out of your head. You need to interrupt the negative stories you keep telling yourself. One of the easiest ways to interrupt your negative self-talk is to go outside and notice what you notice. Chances are, if you walk around outside long enough, you will start to forget to listen to the mean voices in your mind. You might notice someone smiles at you. You might see a beautiful flower or leaf. In the moment when you notice something out in the real world, you begin to work a change deep inside of yourself. You start to melt the thick ice of isolation that has kept you imprisoned inside your mind.

Taking a walk outside is only part of the remedy. You also have to pay attention to what you're seeing. You are only able to pay attention to so much at a time. When you shift your focus from your troubles and onto the world outside, you signal to your brain that it's time to focus on something else. For a little while, your brain exists in troubleshooting mode and enters the more mindful state of noticing. You shift your finite mental resources away from anxiety about the future or past and into a present state of paying attention. If you nourish a habit of going outside where you live and seeing what there is to see, hearing what there is to hear, and smelling what there is to smell, you will start to become mindful, without really trying.

You don't need to become a Zen master or a meditation savant to achieve a sense of peace and mindfulness. All you need is to get outside of your head and head out into the world to notice what you notice. It's always the right time to do something a little weird. If you are unhappy with the way things are going in your life, why should you keep doing things that other people want you to do? You will never get somewhere new until you leave the place where you're currently at. If you want to change your life, you need to be brave enough to get a little weird.

Most of the time, most of us are unaware of anything happening outside of our mental bubble. We go about our days doing our work, running our errands, and complaining about how nobody cares about doing a good job anymore. We completely miss the beautiful smell of new spring grass, the beauty of a birdsong, or the stunning way the sunset looks when reflected in the windows of downtown buildings.

It takes you risking being weird to break out of your default obsession with your own life and problems. It's strange for a full-grown adult to stop in the middle of the sidewalk to take a picture of a sprout pushing through the concrete. It's weird for someone to choose to stop thinking about themselves and start noticing how everyone else is moving around town. But it's always the right time to be a little weird. Nothing wonderful has ever happened without someone first choosing to do something different, something a little weird.

Seeing the world around you, noticing all the things that you are noticing, is weird. It's wonderful. It pulls you out of your problems, helps you relax, and strangely enough, gives you more ideas for how to solve your problems. Have you ever solved a work problem in your dreams or had a brilliant idea in the shower? All of us have had some kind of experience of having an insight when we stopped "thinking" about a problem. Our brains are always working. Human problem-solving, in all of its forms, is a creative act. That means it's a little random, a little mysterious, and one-hundred-percent dependent on gathering enough information from outside of our current collection of facts.

Going outside and noticing stuff gives your brain the raw materials to solve your problems, while also giving you enough space to put all the facts and information you already have together in a new way to generate creative solutions. Going outside with the intention to notice things also allows you to connect more deeply with the plants, animals, people, and environment surrounding you. One challenge is that we are all easily distracted. How do you keep your focus on observing what's happening outside when part of your brain wants to drag you back to stressing about the things you cannot yet solve?

You need to find a way to record your observations. I do this by writing haiku after, or while, taking a walk. I also later draw some of the things I've seen. Sometimes, I take quick pictures with my phone that I can later look through to remember what I saw. Lately, I've also experimented with keeping a weather journal. I write the time of day, the temperature, and a comment or two about the weather. I also try to draw a quick sketch of the sun or clouds. The whole process of the weather journal takes me less than five minutes. But it ensures I get outside, and it keeps me connected to the subtle changes in the seasons.

You need to find a way to record your observations as you brave heading out into the world. It doesn't need to be art. But recording your observations is a kind of creative practice. It's a way to meditate without meditating. You are at your most mindful when noticing, and recording your observations forces you to keep your focus outside of yourself for longer, building your mindfulness muscles.

Ryan Holiday is fond of saying, "I'm not saying going for a walk will solve all your problems, I'm just saying there's no problem that's going to be made worse by going for a walk."

I take things a step further. I'm not saying taking a walk will solve all your problems, but taking regular walks and noticing what you notice will solve some of your problems. Your life changes when you start noticing what is happening outside your window, and you spend less time focused on what's happening in your head.

Chapter 34

Gratitude is Noticing

You and I are walking around with half of our brains shut off. We are essentially sleepwalking through life, preoccupied with worries about things that might never happen and regrets over things that we can never change, while staring into the abyss through our phones five hundred times a day.

When you operate in default mode, letting muscle memory, habits, and prompts from clever marketers guide most of your movements, you become blind to almost everything that's happening in the real world. You don't notice anything. When you fail to pay attention, it's impossible to experience true gratitude because what is gratitude if it's not noticing?

Gratitude is noticing the way nothing hurt when you got out of bed this morning, how the chirping of the sparrows lifts your spirits, and how the smile from the barista in the drive-thru was warm and sincere. Noticing that your car always starts, that you can't remember the last time you had to skip a meal for lack of food, or that your house keeps you dry and warm is gratitude. Gratitude is noticing how heavy your mom's eyelids were as she made you pancakes before school all those years ago.

To be grateful in a world filled with loud noises and bright images designed to lull you into a zombie-like state of constant hustle and consumerism means keeping all of your senses open and your brain fully engaged in the real world, not the virtual dystopia funded, designed, and propped up by plutocrats, kleptocrats, and oligarchs. Being grateful requires you to be awake and an active participant in the real world. It asks you to slow down and notice.

Gratitude isn't about saying please and thank you. It's not keeping a list of things to be grateful for. Gratitude is an awareness of the world around you and the quite small, but important, part you play in the drama of the universe. It's taking the focus off yourself and placing it onto the people, plants, and animals in your environment. It's a holistic practice where you slowly wake up to the fact that you, your thoughts, feelings, moods, and actions are entangled with everything else. You are not a rock. You are not an island. You are a puzzle piece, an ecosystem.

Gratitude is not just a fleeting feeling, like a chill running down your spine or the warmth of a cup of hot chocolate on a winter evening. It is a form of mindfulness. Being grateful and being mindful are inseparable. You cannot be trapped in the past or future and be grateful. You must exist in the present, aware of what is happening, to be grateful. Once you learn to live in the present, you will find that you can look backward and forward and find more things to be grateful for, but your consciousness remains grounded in the right now.

If gratitude and mindfulness are not feelings, what are they? They are practices, they are ways of being. You can think of mindfulness as being made up of a trinity of practices: gratitude, wonder, and calm. However, all of these things, all of these states of being, are entangled. Somehow distinct but inseparable.

MOONBEAMS DANCING OFF
QUAKING,
WET, ORANGE
OAK LEAVES
MIDNIGHT FALL CONCERT

You cannot experience wonder without gratitude and calm. When you achieve a sense of calm, it comes with wonder and gratitude. Gratitude never travels anywhere without calm and wonder. If you want to be mindful, if you want to become more grateful, you must also seek wonder and calm.

Some mistakenly call these things, mindfulness, wonder, calm, and gratitude, virtues. But they are more existential than that. They are a way of living in harmony with your world, while remaining detached enough to notice what is happening. They are a way of becoming the pond and noticing the ripples move through you when the rock momentarily disrupts your surface, as you allow it to pass through.

Noticing then is the path towards gratitude. If you want to be calmer, more filled with wonder, more grateful, and more mindful, you have to start paying attention. You need to wake up.

You build gratitude by noticing a little more each day. You cannot be grateful for what you never see, hear, touch, taste, smell, or experience. Gratitude is built in quiet moments of realization and observation. There are lots of ways to learn how to pay attention. Many use meditation to build a quiet perch from which they can observe their inner world, and then, after much practice, their outer world. Meditation like this has never worked for me. My wiring is too weird for transcendental meditation. But there are many other ways.

Walking around your neighborhood, without your headphones in your ears, and with your phone stashed away in a deep pocket or purse, helps you begin to pay attention.

Author and artist Nishant Jain, known as "The Sneaky Artist," teaches people to keep a secret sketchbook, using it to draw the people and places around them. The goal isn't to become a master draftsman. The goal is to train your brain to pay attention. Sketching in public forces you to see things you never would have noticed before.

THE GREAT
BLUE HERON

FISHING IN THE
SLOW RIVER

WIND PLUCKS OFF
ELM LEAVES

You can also use your phone to build your noticing habit. Instead of opening up your emails, DMs, or infinite social media feed, you can open the camera and take pictures of the tiny wonders you notice as you move around in the world.

In certain parts of the world, you will find mostly older men and women doing tai chi in public parks at dawn. Their disciplined stretching and breathing, outside, helps them see and experience the real world in ways most of us rarely, if ever, achieve.

In college, I knew a woman who loved to walk in forested areas near sunset and dance to the sounds she noticed there. Most people thought she was crazy. While I never thought that, I admit to thinking she was eccentric.Now, more than three decades later, I understand she was right, and I find myself compelled to move to the rhythms I hear in nature, if not as a dance, than as a kind of gentle meandering.

My primary mindfulness practice is writing haiku as I walk in nature or move around town. I love the physicality of counting syllables. Tapping my fingers or quietly clapping my hands, as I make a record of what I'm experiencing. I love to take those poems and turn them into comics, often aided by photos I've taken as a way to memorialize the things I've noticed so that I don't lose track of them.

Choosing to wake up and be present in the world has done more to help me cultivate a deep feeling of gratitude than decades of religious observance and journaling. Gratitude is not something you say, or even something you feel. Gratitude is something you are.

Like every big change, choosing to become grateful requires courage, consistency, and tenderness towards yourself. It's one of those things that you never fully achieve, but one day you notice that something is fundamentally different about the way you now move through the world.

Of course, you are not required to be grateful. You can keep living life the way you've always lived it, half asleep and vulnerable to emotional dysregulation from every piece of bad news or the slightest inconvenience. But, if you have a sense that there's more to life than Slack messages and targeted ads, cultivating gratitude through the power of noticing is your portal to a magical world.

There is never a wrong time to become mindful, grateful. But the best time is today.

I hope that today you're brave enough to stay awake and alert so that you can start your journey to the mystical wonderland of gratitude.

SOME USED TO BELIEVE
BIRDS MIGRATED TO THE MOON
AND SPENT WINTER THERE

Chapter 35

You Aren't Getting Left Behind

Inside my heart and head, I still feel like I'm in my twenties. But my back and the mirror remind me that I'm no longer as bulletproof as I once (thought I) was. I'm now forty-nine, and will hit the half-century mark next year. I'm in the full glory of middle age. I drive slower, am obsessed with birds, and happily dress for comfort instead of, to paraphrase Taylor Swift, dressing for revenge. One of the beauties of this time of life is that I'm no longer worried about getting left behind because I finally understand there's no race. There won't be a finish line, a trophy, and a parade. Life isn't a competition of any kind; I'm not even competing with myself. I'm just a human doing my human thing.

Sometimes, I look back at the anxious, perpetually striving, high-strung young man I was and wonder how I ended up as a middle-aged man who stops to listen to bald eagles I cannot see, trilling in the treetops as I walk by the river; a walk I take not to get fit or to get to any place in particular, but just for the sheer joy of being in nature. The answer, of course, goes back to the way an Earnest Hemingway character in *The Sun Also Rises* describes how he went bankrupt. "Two ways. Gradually, then suddenly."

I'm no longer chasing numbers or approval from gatekeepers, critics, or even family members. It's not that I'm complacent. I'm just content. And, I'm tired of feeling like a rat in a maze, always chasing the scent of cheese, only to find that some god-like figure has moved the cheese and changed the rules of the maze, again.

On social media, I regularly get served ads with dire warnings, asking if I'm someone in my forties or fifties, worried about getting left behind by AI. I'm happy to report that I am not worried about getting left behind by AI, and neither should you be. Each day, it's clearer and clearer that AI is as much of a scam as crypto was. I grew up in Silicon Valley, and I'm the son of a Silicon Valley engineer. I love technology, new gadgets, and am optimistic about the future. But I'm no longer in a hurry to get to that future. It will come in its own time.

Each day, I wake up with a little more gray in my beard, and rushing into the future seems like an even worse idea. In the end, the only thing that's waiting for you and me in the future is death. I'd rather savor my life in this moment. I'm not getting left behind.

You're not getting left behind by AI, your peers, or anything else, either. All the people racing, competing to accumulate the right accomplishments and earn the right amount of money, are running towards the same grave you and I are gently walking towards.

I haven't given up on life. I'm not retired. I still work every day. But through a lot of hard work, luck, and radical change in mindset, I work to make a living from my way of living. I'm fortunate to work for myself, and am not interested in helping anyone else get rich. I just work to make enough money to enjoy life. I take my daily walks, write my poems, draw my pictures, and then put words and pictures together for readers and clients. I'm not interested in doing any of this faster or better than anyone else. My preoccupation is to make cool stuff that is true to my soul, and is the best I can make at the time.

This life of contentment is possible for you, too. But you have to be willing to drop out of the sprint/marathon society wants you to run. You have to stop regretting the past and agonizing over the uncertain future. Instead of always trying to get somewhere in your professional and personal lives, you need to learn to just be. Contentment comes from noticing the current moment and learning to stay there.

The problem with seeing life as a race or competition is that someone has to lose, or more likely, several people. The life-as-a-competition model creates a pyramid with a narrow clique of "winners" at the top, supported by a massive base of "losers" at the bottom. Billionaire oligarchs love stoking the competitive flames of the base, reaping all the benefits of increased productivity, grinding the rest of us, their workers, to dust. The idea that life is some kind of competition is not unique to the US or the West, but it feels more pronounced here.

FALL WINDS
BREAK UP
CLOUDS

REVEALING
PALE BLUE
SKY,

OUR
RESOLUTE SUN

In American folklore, two stories highlight the tension we often feel between new technologies and the desire to preserve a way of life. John Henry and Paul Bunyan both fought automation and lost. John Henry was the greatest steel driver on the railroad construction site until a new machine turned up, which was faster than even Henry, at least according to the machine's inventor. Henry raced the machine, and even though in some versions of the tale he won the race, his heart exploded from the exertion, killing him. Paul Bunyan was a giant lumberjack who was a pillar of his community until a salesman showed up with a new steam saw. Bunyan and the steam-saw-wielding salesman entered into a competition to see who could cut the most lumber. Bunyan narrowly lost. He went into exile, searching for new frontiers until he disappeared. The lessons from the folktales are clear. Progress is inevitable, and resisting the machines will kill you.

But this is all a lie. We get to decide what progress means. We don't have to adopt AI, or any other technology that makes life worse for most people. Once you realize that not only are you likely to lose any race you compete in, but that you don't even need to enter the race at all, you start to see the world differently.

Life isn't about waiting for something good to happen to you. It's about seeing the good already happening all around you right now. You can get joy from the process of writing, instead of racing to see how fast you can get an article out. You don't need to chase virality. We all need to pay the bills, but you can take pride in whatever work you do without wishing your life away.

I've been self-employed virtually my whole life. For most of that time, I've traded hours for dollars, and there's nothing wrong with that. I've been a working writer for more than thirteen years, and outside of the last nine months, I've always made the vast majority of my money working for clients instead of from my "art". I've watched dozens of colleagues chase passive income and race to build a creative business so they could write full-time. All of them have burned out and quit creating art of any kind.

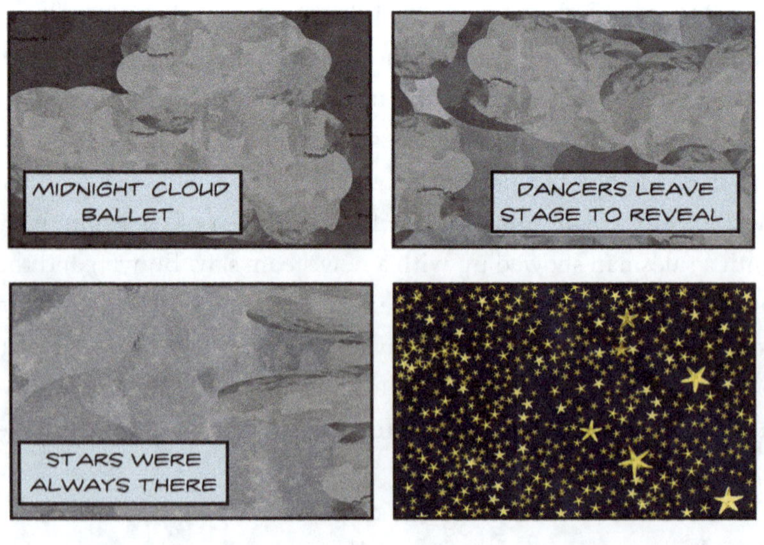

Meanwhile, I've moved forward with my weird poetry comics at a glacial pace. Refusing to rush and loving every minute of the creative process, even when nobody else seemed to care about what I was creating. I don't have a niche, I'm not rich, and I have no desire to sell you a system, playbook, or blueprint.

I started making poetry comics in 2019, and this year is the first year where the majority of my income is from my creative work, instead of client work. However, I still need client work to pay all the bills and have enough money to live comfortably. There's nothing wrong with that! I love working with my clients. I still need that day job. There were many moments when I wondered if I was getting left behind as I watched other writers and artists go viral and make loads of money. But they all dropped out of creative life. Since I never entered the race, I never lost, I never had to quit.

I sometimes wonder if it's even possible for young people to understand that life isn't a race. Perhaps, you have to live enough life to learn that you can slow down and enjoy life, that knowing what birds match what sounds gives life a rich texture. Then I pay attention to what my Gen Z kids are doing and saying. They are teens and young adults, and they are so much wiser than I was at their ages. They get it. They seem to intuitively understand the lessons embedded in Gex X movies like *War Games* and *Ferris Bueller's Day Off*. Both of these movies star a young Matthew Broderick playing a precocious teenager in conflict with authority.

In *War Games*, Broderick's character almost starts, and then helps stop, a global thermonuclear war by learning, and then teaching a supercomputer, that in some games, the only winning move is to never start the game. In his turn as the titular Ferris Bueller, Matthew Broderick breaks the fourth wall to tell the audience, "Life moves pretty fast. If you don't stop and look around once in a while, you could miss it."

Gen Z is showing that they aren't willing to sacrifice their lives to play as pawns in someone else's game. But the rest of us still need to internalize these lessons. The next time you find yourself falling into the trap of hustling and grinding until you die, ask yourself, where are you in such a hurry to get to? Why are you running in someone else's race? You aren't getting left behind. Stop, breathe, and listen to the birds. Your best life is happening right now; you just need to be still enough to notice it.

Chapter 36

The Case for Regrets

I don't know when I first learned the Latin phrase *carpe diem*. I know it was before the phrase was a major theme in the 1989 Robin Williams movie *Dead Poets Society*. Carpe diem —seize the day—was in the zeitgeist during my teenage years. I learned carpe diem before my friends and I sat in the lobby of an orthodontist's office one Friday night, waiting for Eric to finish his evening cleaning duties at the place where his mom worked as an office manager. This was the only kind of nepotism we experienced in our social circle.

Eric came out from the back with a white box, gleefully telling Chip he was holding Robyn's dental impressions. Chip grabbed the box, pulled out a plaster mold of Robyn's teeth, raised it above his head as if it were Excalibur, and proclaimed, "Carpe dentum!" Sending us all sprawling with laughter.

Eric asked for the box back, but it had somehow disappeared. We high school boys may have all known a single Latin phrase, but none of us understood medical privacy. (HIPAA was still two years away from becoming the law of the land.)

In today's youth-centric culture, you rarely hear that dusty

Latin phrase. It's largely been replaced with YOLO—you only live once. In some circles, you also hear two words that make me shudder. No regrets.

It seems the only thing we fear more than death as a culture is living a life filled with regret. It's common to believe that regrets are the mark of an unfulfilling life and that you will regret more the things you didn't do than the ones you did. However, this idea of no regrets tends to be an excuse for being an asshole. I am suspicious of any adult who proudly proclaims that they have no regrets in life. This is only possible in two dire circumstances. Either you have lived a life so cautious and insular that you have never done anything worth remembering, or you have never matured enough to understand other people's emotions.

It is not possible to live in this world and love others without also causing injury to others. To love is to open yourself to the heartache of hurting those you love and the heartbreak of love not being reciprocated. To love is to live a life that will lead to regrets. A regret is simply the realization of having made a mistake. Regrets are how our brains and souls keep us from repeating the same mistake.

Regrets are separate from shame. Shame is an emotion that keeps you trapped in the past, preventing you from growing and evolving. Regrets are a tool for living in the present moment, taking a memory of the past to keep you anchored in the now.

Henry David Thoreau said, "To regret deeply is to live afresh." Thoreau knew something of regret, having once accidentally started a raging wildfire that put many of his neighbors and their crops in jeopardy.

Your regrets allow you to become a new person. Instead of stopping you from living a full life, regrets allow you to transform into the person you want to be. They are a tool for living your most human life.

My biggest regrets from my youth all stem from how I treated other people's feelings. I was timid when I should've been bold—reckless when I should've been tender. The relationships I failed to pursue out of fear are some of the most vibrant memories from the days of loitering in the orthodontist's office after hours. I hurt people who had some love for me because I was too timid to show my love. However, the memories that shape my behavior and character the most as I approach 50, even more than the loves lost to my lack of boldness, are the times I hurt people through my thoughtless and reckless words.

I've always had a quick wit and a sharp tongue—survival instincts from a childhood filled with fear, bullying, and abuse. It took me far too long to understand that my words could cut others deeply. I had to learn how to be tender with the emotions of others, having few role models from the adults closest to me. Too many times, I hurt someone not because I was intentionally cruel but because I was trying to be funny. But, just like a sharp blade cuts when it comes into contact with your skin, regardless of the intention of the wielder, harsh words scar even if the purpose is not malevolent.

I have forgiven myself for the foolish boy I was. I don't carry shame over my past, but I do carry regrets. Those regrets continue to help me become the man I want to be. My regrets are tools to help me close the gap between my current self and my ideal self. Regrets help me to love more deeply, live more honestly, and laugh more openly. While shame once chained me to living in the past, regrets free me to live in the present. Regrets are a kind of mindfulness nudge.

The idea of trying to live a life with no regrets can also lead you into a life of perfectionism, where your biggest fear is doing the wrong thing, so you do nothing. The Gen Z fear of being "cringe", a fear that is certainly not limited to Gen Z, but a fear people of all generations carry, is about avoiding doing anything too earnest, or anything someone stranger on the internet might think is stupid.

If you are afraid of regretting doing something cringe, you rob yourself of the chance to connect with other weird humans who share, or love, your passions and eccentricities. You live a stunted life, encased in bubble wrap, outwardly smug about your lack of regrets and cringey behavior, while slowly dying on the inside. I strive to live each day to the fullest. That means working on showing up in the world as my truest self. Being fully human.

Being my earnest, cringey self. Being fully human means constantly falling short of my loftiest ideals.

Failure is a reason to celebrate. It is a sign that I am living. I am not hoping to optimize my life. Instead, I accept my fallibility and work to help others instead of hurting them and to do the same for myself. When I make a mistake, I apologize; I learn from it and allow that mistake to inform my future choices. Someone who has lived a life with no regrets is someone who is not honest with themself or others. They are too weak to accept accountability and too cowardly to live a great life. No regrets is no kind of life.

The next time you consider the idea of carpe diem or YOLO, allow your regrets to push you towards a more fulfilling, gentle, and meaningful present. In the end, we are all flawed. All we can do is be gracious with ourselves and others and become more curious and kind as we age. Move slowly and fix things.

Author's Note

Each essay in this collection was published between February 2024 and December 2025 on Medium.com and my *Weirdo Poetry* newsletter (weirdopoetry.substack.com). Some of the newsletter posts and all of the Medium essays are paywalled. All the essays appearing here have been revised and altered. In some cases the titles have also been changed. The poetry comics featured in these essays all debuted in my *Weirdo Poetry* newsletter, though many are appearing in with revised art and altered formats.

I have published two collections of haiku comics, *Wild Divinity* and *Haiku Comics from the Anthropocene*. Most of the haiku comics in this book are adapted from versions published in those collections. The *Haiku Robot* comics found in Chapter 17 and Chapter 19 are from a limited series I originally published in my *Weirdo Poetry* newsletter and then republished on Medium.

I've been making poetry comics in one form or another since the COVID pandemic in 2020. They have become my primary creative outlet, and they are what I think of as my real work. However, it is my illustrated essays that have garnered the most attention. My illustrated essays are what allowed me to make a real living as a poet-cartoonist, which is funny because I only started making essays illustrated with poetry comics as a kind of Trojan Horse for the poetry comics. It was a way to sneak them into people's feeds.

I'm not sure if it worked or not, but I've become committed to the craft of making these illustrated essays even as I continue making poetry comics, and break ground on a few different fiction projects. My *Weirdo Poetry* newsletter has not only been a wonderful creative laboratory, but it has also helped me find a wonderful community of poets, writer, and artists on Substack.

One of my friends, and one of my favorite Subtackers, is Ann Collins. She writes *Microseasons* (72seasons.substack.com). In the third essay in this book, *Daytripping,* I use a lengthy excerpt from her newsletter with her permission. Originally, the Collins quote and surrounding paragraphs appeared in a *Weirdo Poetry* newsletter issue titled, *Sheryl Crow Weather*. It was more of a sketch rather than a proper essay. The essay *Daytripping* was written around the same time, but I never had a satisfying way to end it. Taking a page from Paul McCartney, I smashed two essays together, to make something much stronger and interesting that either piece was on their own.

In chapter 24, I have a collage illustration that uses costume designs of Alice and the Cheshire Cat made by John Tenniel in 1915 for a production of *Alice in Wonderland* that never has produced. However, his costume designs are iconic and heavily influenced every theatrical and cinematic adaptation of the works of Lewis Carol that came afterward.

Chapter 28, *How to be a Sea Turtle* references Emily Nunn's wonderful newsletter, *The Department of Salad.* It can be found at https://emilyrnunn.substack.com/.

I love hearing from readers. The best way to reach me is either through my website, *WeirdoPoetry.com* or by joining my *Weirdo Poetry* newsletter and replying to my posts.

Thank you for reading this collection of illustrated essays. I hope it helps you think more deeply about what it means to be human. Now, go and be the weird you want to see in the world!

About the Author

Jason McBride is an author of multiple books and zines. He is a poet, illustrator, and amateur human.

When he's not making poetry comics, he can be found on the beach, walking near the river, or hiking in the mountains.

Join the *Weirdo Poetry* newsletter, and each week you will get a free issue with poetry comics and illustrated thoughts about living a slow, human life through poetry and walking.

SCAN ME

weirdopoetry.substack.com

instagram.com/weirdo_poetry

youtube.com/@weirdopoetry